The SAT®
STRATEGY
GUIDEBOOK

A TEACHING and SELF-INSTRUCTION guide to mastering the SAT through key strategies and techniques.

☐ Prepared in ready-to-teach lesson-plan format – Ideal for SAT Instructors
☐ Including: Quizzes/Post-test to measure student mastery of strategies and techniques!
☐ Featuring the strategic "Karelitz approach" to maximizing SAT-scores!

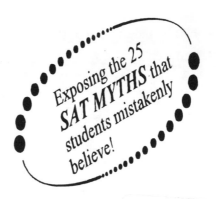

Exposing the 25 SAT MYTHS that students mistakenly believe!

Raymond Karelitz
B.A./Ed.B/M.A.

D1303573

HI-LITE PUBLISHING COMPANY
P.O. Box 240161
Honolulu, Hawaii 96824

©2000
website: www. mixinblender.com

Copyright© 2000 by HI-LITE PUBLISHING COMPANY
P.O. Box 240161, Honolulu, Hawaii 96824

"Scholastic Assessment Test," **SAT®**, **PSAT®** and **TWS®** are registered trademarks of the College
Board. The information contained herein does not necessarily reflect the views of or is endorsed
by any organization other than the publishers of this book. Information regarding the SAT should
be directed to the College Board, Princeton, New Jersey 08541.

Mr. Raymond Karelitz is the creator of the *HI-LITE Series© Vocabulary Program,* an innovative
approach which has helped students throughout the country build vocabulary skills essential for
communication.

In addition to his verbal expertise, Mr. Karelitz scored a perfect 800 on the Graduate Record
Exam (SAT) Math, which he took "just to see what it would be like."

He currently teaches classes and workshops throughout his home-state of Hawaii.

 Computer-Processing & Layout: Barbara Bower

Cartoons: James Makashima

Cover Design: Doug Behrens
Back-Cover Photo by: Vince Rodrigues

Library of Congress Catalog Card Number: 99-98139

Library of Congress Cataloguing-in-Publication Data
Karelitz, Raymond 1952-
    The SAT Strategy Guidebook
      1. Scholastic assessment test – Study guides. I. Title.

ISBN: 1-56391-010-1
Printed in the United States of America

Table of Contents

Page

Preface 3-6

A General Look at Colleges & the **SAT** 7-11

Maximum **SAT** Scoring 12

The **SAT** Verbal Section: An Overview 13

SAT Sentence Completions 14-25

SAT Analogies 26-41

SAT Reading 42-59

Final Thought (Verbal) 59

The **SAT** Math Section: An Overview 60-65

SAT Math Multiple Choice Problems 66-85

SAT Math Quantitative Comparison Problems 86-101

SAT Math Student-Produced Answer Problems 102-114

Final Thought (Math) 114

Final Overview Note on the **SAT** 115-116

The **PSAT** Test of Writing Skills 117-131

Final Thought (TWS) 131

Overview: Suggestions to Build **SAT** Skills 132

A Closing Note 133-134

Concise Review: Strategic "Karelitz Approach" 135-136

Concise Review: Maximum **SAT** Scoring 137-138

Challenging **SAT** Final Exam 139-177

Final Exam Answers 178

Final Exam Scoring Worksheet and Chart 179-180

Strategy-Review Checklist 181

Troubleshooting 182-183

Recommended Books/Video/Computer Program 184

Words Most Often Appearing on the **SAT** 185-203

Index 204-205

Preface

There are many different SAT books on the market, most of which are pretty much the same. They all discuss the history of the SAT and explain how important the test is. Then they look at each part of the test and give the same directions with the same general advice. They are good texts for introducing the reader to the SAT but they don't tell you more than what you probably already know. The thicker the book, the more gobbledygook it tends to contain. Rather than wading through these tedious texts, you are probably better off getting a sample SAT from your high school counselor and seeing for yourself just how high you can score. The book made by the College Board (the makers of the actual SAT) contains samples of past tests and is an excellent source for practice tests. By practicing and reviewing your errors, you will probably learn more about the test than by reading through hundreds of pages of general explanations.

The one big problem about nationally-popular SAT books is that they have built their reputation on the company names they represent. But I have discovered that the larger the company name, the less helpful the text seems to be in addressing individual needs. The books instead tend to be geared toward the same audience: those who are already quite familiar with the test and are already quite test-wise. When it comes to addressing problems encountered by students who really need to get "minimum" scores, those books fall flat. It's easy to brag about students who have raised their scores to 1300 after reading the book or taking the national classes, but is this really a dramatic feat for those who already began at 1050? A more challenging endeavor is to try to help students scoring 750 to raise their scores to 1000; few, if any, of the "big guns" have targeted this audience. The simple fact is that the large companies who have been teaching the same methods for a hundred years don't know how to reach the "ordinary" teenager.

My first two SAT books (*Understanding the SAT in 10 Easy Lessons* and *The New SAT in 10 Easy Steps*) presented simple, understandable strategies for those weak in their SAT scores. Additional tips and explanations were added to better help improve scores, and the results were dramatic. The *SAT Strategy Guidebook* is my latest contribution, with more key strategies for conquering the dreaded SAT!

SAT Textbooks and SAT Classes:
Perpetuating the Same Inequalities

Most SAT books on the market are long and boring, others are too technical and therefore not understandable. Perhaps that's why SAT-preparation classes have flourished over the past few years; it's easier to have someone "walk you through" the test than read through confusing explanations on your own. Unfortunately, you pay for that service, and the results aren't always worth the investment. With larger companies, the teachers often structure their lessons around the boring texts published by the firms; in effect, you're paying to have another person read to you what neither fully understands. Where's the logic in that? Again, those who benefit are those who already know the test or can afford hundreds of dollars for lengthy test-prep courses. Those academically and socioeconomically at a disadvantage – those who desperately need to be given an equal chance – are the very ones left to fend for themselves or fall farther behind.

In the Beginning....

There was a time when I believed the SAT was an aptitude test and that "smart" students would always outscore the rest. But then I wondered why so many academically gifted adolescents were not scoring well on their SATs. I knew there was something they were not understanding about the test, so I began to write my own SAT books to address the problem. While writing these earlier editions, I also began to realize that if these students could raise their scores, why couldn't everyone?! What began as a germinal thought back then has, years later, evolved into *The SAT Strategy Guidebook*. It represents the latest SAT-approach to building scores from the ground up and gives everyone an even chance to excel on the SAT!

About the Author

I have been teaching SAT-preparation courses for over fifteen years; before that, I tutored SAT-prep for half a dozen. During this time, I have also written several articles on the basic structure of the SAT and on strategic approaches toward mastering the test. One thing I have never done is follow a traditional approach or assume that any single approach will ever stand the test of time and change. My SAT-prep classes are always changing focus, the strategies constantly being adjusted to best meet the ever-changing audience. In my home-state of Hawaii, my classes – which reach over 3000 students annually – now include parents and teachers in attendance. The hands-on approach, together with my strategic test-taking fine-tuning, has led to student gains of over 300 points in as little as one month! More importantly, these gains have been not by students who have gone home and studied day and night but by normal students who have simply gained test-taking strategic skills sufficient to generate dramatic results. Many of these students have received scholarships as a result of their improvement (academic and athletic scholarships often require a minimum SAT score to qualify), and countless others have been able to get into the college of their choice due to the increased scores. My approach pinpoints student weaknesses and develops a plan of attack to shore up these pitfalls. And because many of my students are Seniors, I have been forced to integrate within the plan a method for achieving MAXIMUM results with MINIMUM effort and in a MINIMUM of time. In other words, many of my students have only one chance left – it's "do or die." The results have been so encouraging that I have at last felt it time to share this latest "magic formula" with the rest of the world. What you now have before you is no ordinary book; it is the key to opening doors to your future!

Let's Get Going

If you feel confident that you can raise your SAT scores, then you're ready to walk through this book with me as your guide. If you still don't feel you can handle the SAT, consider this: The SAT is a test made for 8th graders, not high schoolers! There is <u>nothing</u> on the test that any student with common sense can't master. In fact, at this point you are probably at the same test-wise level as most others your age; your potential simply needs to be channeled in the right direction to fully demonstrate your capability.

Here's a question to ponder, and I doubt that one person in ten knows the correct answer:

The SAT is primarily a(n) _____ test.
- (A) aptitude
- (B) multiple-choice
- (C) vocabulary
- (D) reading
- (E) standardized
- (F) time-management

Once you understand what the answer really is, you will begin to see just what the SAT is all about. It is at that moment your scores will begin to rise steadily!

A Note to Keep in Mind...

This is not an SAT book; it is a book of <u>test-taking</u>. Its approach will open your eyes to your potential on any test, whether it be multiple choice, true/false or essay. Test-taking is an art, not a science! You can generate "beautiful" scores without being an Einstein; all it takes is an open mind and the confidence that you can succeed. While other books boast of having readers get near-perfect scores (which isn't a far cry from their beginning scores of 1400+), this book can boast of a much greater achievement: One student who followed the strategic plan of attack raised his Math score 200 points (280 to 480) in three weeks. It enabled him to be able to play football at a Division I college. Ten months later, he was selected as Conference Freshman of the Year. And now, he plays in the NFL. Whenever he's back home, he drops by and never fails to remind me that the SAT Math score played a large part in bringing him to where he is today. If he can do it, so can you!

I don't want to forget the other end of the spectrum. I have been coaching a younger student since he was in the seventh grade. He has been a prime beneficiary of the ever-improving strategies, and his scores have improved since the first time he took the test. Now a Sophomore, his latest combined score was 1410, quite an increase from his 890 three years ago. He is a fine example of the upper potential of this strategic plan of attack: He hopes to get a 1600 in his junior year, and I believe he has a very good chance to do so. Because of the success of this new "plan of attack," he has dubbed it the "Karelitz approach," a term I may find in greater popularity as the results come in!

Keep in mind that a good test score is simply a product of mastering the basics of test-taking; the more time one has to develop these skills, the higher one can climb. There is no limit (other than 1600) as to how high you can soar on the SAT if you begin your SAT journey early in your high school career. I hope you've got your running shoes on, because you're about to embark on a mission towards a future that is only bounded by your own ambition. From this point on, there's nothing holding you back. Let the journey begin.

THE KEYS TO SUCCESS.... IN COLLEGE
AND BEYOND:

1. DESIRE TO SUCCEED!
(EFFORT IS MORE IMPORTANT
THAN TALENT!)

2. DEPENDABILITY!
(COMPLETE ALL ASSIGNMENTS
ON TIME... EARLY, IF POSSIBLE!)

7

A General (and Brief) Look at Colleges and the SAT

Generally, colleges only look upon the SAT as a standardized test that enables them to compare student scores on a nationwide basis. There are other ingredients in a student's high school life that mean more to colleges than the SAT:

1st) COURSE-selection is oftentimes the most important ingredient to colleges, especially the more-select ones. Honors and Advanced Placement courses are highly valued, as are specialty-courses such as Band, ROTC, advanced Language, advanced Sciences, advanced Math, business, computer, psychology and advanced Art classes. In short, colleges want to see a challenging high school curriculum; many require it.

2nd) ACTIVITIES/CLUBS show colleges the extent of your interests and commitments as well as leadership skills and individual responsibility. Many colleges seek out students who are actively involved in sports, drama, journalism, yearbook, school newspaper, student government or other related activities. Membership in clubs is highly regarded by colleges; having leadership roles in clubs is even more impressive. Colleges recognize that the leaders of tomorrow are most likely in leadership positions today – are you one of them?

3rd) The SAT comes in 3rd place, not 1st as many SAT instructors may have you believe. However, the SAT can prove to be a mighty barrier if the scores are too low.

Let's examine all the factors that can attract colleges; see which "trump cards" you hold:
- HIGH-QUALITY COURSES
- STRONG GRADE-POINT-AVERAGE (B or higher)
- SPORTS/BAND/DRAMA/ROTC – college "specialties" – especially when special honors have been received
- LEADERSHIP achievements – especially when community commendation has been bestowed
- ETHNIC BACKGROUND – a bonanza for scholarships and grants if you qualify
- OUTSTANDING SAT (or ACT) scores

Of these six "trump cards," which do you think is easiest to add to your "hand"? Courses, grades and activities/achievements do not materialize overnight; adding these cards to your hand requires time and commitment. Because ethnic background is pre-determined, this is a card you cannot add if it isn't already in your "hand." Only the SAT represents a "card" you have immediate control to improve your "hand" with. Simply learn the ropes of SAT test-taking and the results can be both sudden and dramatic. No other "trump card" can be so easily obtained and used in your favor!

The SAT is thus the only college-requirement that can be satisfied in one day. This is why many students plan ahead and take the SAT in their Sophomore and then again in their Junior years. It only takes one good score to satisfy this requirement; no other "trump card" can be attained so quickly. In addition, because this test covers very basic content-matter, waiting until you are a Junior or Senior can actually prove detrimental to your success.

> • MYTH #1: It is better to begin preparing for the SAT in one's Junior year.

> • FACT: The sooner you begin preparing for the SAT, the better you will do.

I have found, with few exceptions, that the earlier a student begins preparing for the SAT, the better the student performs on the test. For example, in my classes I have Freshmen, Sophomores, Juniors and Seniors enrolled. Few if any have had previous experience with the SAT; many don't even know that it is basically the same test as the PSAT, though longer. What I have noticed is that the Sophomores score higher on our practice tests than any other group; next are the Juniors and Freshmen. Seniors run a consistent last of all four grade-levels! The later you start, the lower your SAT starting score-level is likely to be. (MYTH #1 is but one of many MYTHS people have regarding the SAT; I will highlight other myths as our investigation progresses.) Therefore, begin as early as you can (today is a good time to start!) and you will see your SAT score begin to rise on Day 1 and continue rising from that day on!

Remember that COURSES, GRADES and ACTIVITIES play a major role for those wishing to join the ranks of the college crowd. This book, however, will focus on gaining the upper hand on the other "trump card": the SAT.

Maximum **SAT** Scoring: Know What To Do (and what not to do)

• MYTH #2: If you don't know an answer, skip it.

> • FACT: You should try to answer as many questions as possible, even those you are not absolutely certain about.

Despite the penalty imposed on the SAT for wrong answers (a fractional amount, hardly worth mentioning), the fact is that SAT scoring is based on the number you get CORRECT. If you don't answer a question, you cannot possibly get it correct.

• MYTH #3: A person begins with a 200 as soon as the test begins.

> • FACT: A person begins with an <u>800</u> as soon as the test begins.

Every student begins the test with a perfect score (800); however, from that point on you LOSE points for every problem not answered correctly. So if you skip a problem, you LOSE – approximately 10 points; if you get it wrong, you LOSE – approximately 12 ½ points. If you decide to skip 20 problems, you have ensured a loss of 200 points before the scoring has even begun. And for those who want to compare skipping 20 problems with getting 20 wrong, here are the grisly results:

SKIP 20: you LOSE 200 points
GET 20 WRONG: you LOSE 250 points

Which is worse? For the answer to this, first answer the following question (the answers are the same): What would you rather cut off, your right leg or your left leg? The answer is simple: NEITHER. You want to keep them both. On the SAT, you don't want to LOSE – whether it's 200 or 250 points.

The strategy for maximum scoring on the SAT is very simple: Don't skip if at all possible. Get as many correct as you can. On problems you are unsure about, you'll need to acquaint yourself with the test-takers' closest ally: test strategies.

...And that's what this book is all about!

The **SAT** VERBAL Section (The Test We Love to Hate): An Overview

The SAT contains three types of Verbal problems:
SENTENCE COMPLETIONS (fill-in-the-blanks)
ANALOGIES (word-relationships)
READING questions

- MYTH #4: The SAT is a vocabulary test.

- FACT: The SAT is no longer a vocabulary test.

Ask anyone who took the SAT twenty years ago and you're sure to hear that its main focus is on vocabulary. That was true then; it is not true any longer. More than half the test-questions are now focused on the READING passages. Vocabulary really only plays a significant role in the harder SENTENCE COMPLETIONS and ANALOGIES problems, of which there aren't many. Building your vocabulary is a worthwhile activity, not so much for improving SAT scores as for increasing your personal word-power. Vocabulary is a powerful tool; others measure you by the words you use. A person with a strong vocabulary will find many more doors of opportunity opening.

On the SAT, vocabulary plays a minor role. Frankly, it is not worthwhile studying vocabulary lists if your aim is to improve your SAT score to moderate levels: 450-500. There are easier, quicker ways to raise your SAT scores. Simply put, studying vocabulary for SAT improvement is generally a waste of time! Much as I love exploring and analyzing the eclectic array and wondrousness of words, I cannot recommend what does not translate favorably onto SAT test-scores. There are much more effective ways to raise test-scores; however, for those who prefer to rely on knowledge rather than strategies, I welcome you to stop reading this book and proceed immediately to a word-building textbook. If you've got the time and determination, you will find the results well worth the effort. For the rest of us mortals, however, I encourage you to put away your dictionaries and read on.

SAT SENTENCE COMPLETIONS:
The Only Part of the SAT That is Not Worth the Time and Effort!

> • MYTH #5: Each problem on the SAT is worth the same.

>> • FACT: Problems on the SAT are <u>not</u> all worth the same.

This is an intriguing fact, considering that theoretically all SAT problems are scored equally. To better explain why they really aren't all of equal value, let's back up a bit and look at the test as a whole. The SAT Verbal and Math sections are constructed in a carefully planned order: The first few problems are usually the easiest and the final few are usually the hardest. (The Reading section is the only exception, but that will be discussed later.)

> • MYTH #6: The last (hardest) problems are worth the most points.

No, this isn't true either. In fact, the first few, <u>easiest</u> problems are worth the most! Ponder this for a moment. Confused? Well, you shouldn't be. Ask yourself what your main goal is when you take the SAT. Is it to learn something? No. Is it to get into your favorite college? That may be an ultimate goal but not the goal while you're taking the SAT. There's only one goal at this time: to get a good score. More specifically, you want to achieve the best score you possibly can. And how can you reach this optimal score? By getting as many questions correct as you can. Of course, not all the questions are of equal difficulty; so where do you have the best chance to get correct answers? At the <u>beginning</u>, where the problems are easiest to answer right.

>> • FACT: The easiest problems on the SAT are worth the most because you can get them correct!

Having clarified how to maximize your score, let's examine briefly the worst thing you could do that would seriously reduce your chances of maximizing your score. I'm sure you have an answer, but you're probably wrong. The real answer brings us to a clarification of a point raised earlier, that skipping is the worst thing you can do on the SAT. In fact, there is something worse, even though we do know how disastrous skipping can be.

An Eye-Opening Revelation

The SAT Verbal tests are approximately 30 minutes per section. Each section begins with approximately 10 SENTENCE COMPLETIONS, then progresses to 6-13 ANALOGIES and winds up with a READING passage accompanied by a group of related questions. Similar to a football game, the SAT can be approached with a variety of game-plans and strategies. These must, however, be fully utilized within a set period of time. When the clock runs out, the "game" is over.

The goal in a football game is to execute strategic plans of attack to perfection, thereby scoring as many points possible to ensure victory. Each tactic has its purpose: to contribute to the main goal. The goal on an SAT is much the same: to utilize all strategies available to maximize the score.

What is the worst position a football team can find themselves in? What one factor can stymie even the best of strategic plans of attack? It is the same factor that can cripple even the best-laid plans of the SAT-attack: lack of time. The worst thing you can do on the SAT is waste time! Spending too much time on any one question is a recipe for disaster; getting that problem wrong even after spending too much time is double-disaster.

On the SENTENCE COMPLETIONS, where do you feel you might find yourself likely to spend more time? Most likely it will be on the final few, difficult sentences. Do you plan to get these final problems correct? Probably not. So why are you wasting valuable time on problems that you don't expect to get correct!

On the SAT Verbal section, where is the time most needed? It does not seem to be critical on the SENTENCE COMPLETIONS portion, where the easier problems can be answered quickly and the harder ones will remain hard even if you had an hour to spend on them. Time is your most precious possession when you reach the READING section, because it is here that you can use it constructively. The more time you have to read a passage and answer the questions, the higher your score is likely to be. The worst-case scenario is when a student tells me he didn't have enough time to adequately read and answer the questions at the end of the section. Now we know what he did wrong. Don't put yourself in this position.

Strategic "Karelitz Approach": SENTENCE COMPLETIONS

The first thing to do on a SENTENCE COMPLETION is to read the sentence. It may sound obvious, but there are those who feel they can "fit" the choices right into the sentence. Fact is, all the choices "fit" but only one makes sense. Reading the sentence first will give you an idea of the general thought that is being conveyed in the sentence.

The next step is oftentimes overlooked, and skipping this step can cause avoidable mistakes. After having read the sentence, take a moment (not a minute, just a moment) to place your own words into the blank(s). Substitute an easy word in the blank that completes the thought. Don't look at the choices yet; wait until you have a good idea what you are looking for. Key words in the sentence will alert you to whether a word is going to be a "good" or a "bad" word, and when there are two blanks whether they may be similar or opposite to one another. Reading the sentence and inserting your own words will help you greatly to determine which of the five choices is the BEST answer by ELIMINATING the choices that do not make sense.

"Limited Elimination": A Very Effective Strategy

Whenever a multiple choice test asks for the BEST answer, the most successful way to arrive at the answer is by eliminating two or three choices. What you will have left are only two or three remaining choices from which to pick your BEST answer, and it's much easier to select the correct one when there are only a couple of choices left. Don't try to eliminate all four choices; it usually isn't worth the extra time and effort. The LIMITED ELIMINATION strategy is the most efficient approach, given the factor of time: Eliminate two or three choices, select from what is left, and move on. Remember also that you should always write in the test booklet. Don't eliminate "in your head." Cross off those that are eliminated and you will find fewer careless errors as a result.

Key Words & The "Morass"

SENTENCE COMPLETIONS problems are not difficult, but vocabulary becomes a real hazard as they progress. In those all-important easy ones (at the beginning), look for key words that signal the main thought of the sentence. For example: "In her youth, she was _____: she had friends wherever she lived." In this sentence, the main idea is restated after the colon-punctuation (the ":"): "she had friends wherever she lived." The next step is to place your own word into the blank: She could have been "popular" or "well-liked" or "friendly." Any of these words give you an idea as to what you are seeking, and once you have this step completed, the rest is simple.

Theoretically, even the more difficult sentences are easy to answer if you follow these three simple steps: READ, CREATE YOUR OWN ANSWER, REVIEW THE CHOICES FOR ONE THAT FITS/ELIMINATE THOSE THAT DON'T. But the following sample will illustrate the underlying problem: "In his profligacy, he was not one to _____." The sentence is short and rather easy to understand if you know what "profligacy" means. It's clear that the blank is the opposite of "profligacy," but again it's a matter of knowing the word; if you know what "profligacy" means, this problem is easy. But for most of us, vocabulary is the rub that adversely affects SENTENCE COMPLETION success and invariably hurts SAT scores; SENTENCE COMPLETIONS are by far the most consistently weak portion of the SAT Verbal. In addition, it is because of the difficulty of the harder SENTENCE COMPLETIONS problems that many remember the SAT as primarily a vocabulary test. We know, however, that this in not true because only one quarter of the test consists of these problems (thank goodness!).

Getting Out of the Morass

So far, we've discovered that the first few SENTENCE COMPLETIONS problems are quite easy and the final ones are vocabulary-difficult. In an attempt to maximize SAT score-results, what is your best plan of attack on this section? Your goal remains the same: Get as many problems correct as you can (using the "limited elimination" approach) and don't waste time. Therefore, it is imperative that you work quickly on this section. So what should you do when the pace begins to slow (in other words, when vocabulary begins to bog you down)? The one thing not to do is spend much time on the final few sentences. They are not worth as much as the first ones (because you probably won't get them correct!), so why spend precious time when you could be applying it more successfully on the READING section! Try to answer the questions through some sort of elimination, but consider these final few sentences as "hit-or-miss." Don't be concerned if you might have gotten them wrong; few people get them right, anyway. Your concern should be to get through quickly and to get the first half correct. Anything correct after that is simply "icing on the cake."

Seeking Perfection

For most students, getting half of the SENTENCE COMPLETIONS problems correct will suffice. However, if you are one of the few whose goal it is to attain a Verbal score over 650, then it is vital that you have a solid vocabulary. To earn a score of 650 or more, you cannot afford to have a weak section on the Verbal; getting half of the SENTENCE COMPLETIONS problems correct will not suffice. There are several ways to build vocabulary; some are fun, others are more "learning-oriented."

1) FUN: Crossword Puzzles. My favorite puzzles are those that focus on SAT words. Most of the ones you see in newspapers are geared for experts and contain a potpourri of questions ranging from history to Greek mythology. They are not puzzles you want to spend time on if your focus is on SAT vocabulary-building. The best puzzles are found in your local supermarket in the magazine section. Penny Press Publications are the best for SAT-words. Their crossword puzzle titles sound easy – "Good Time Crossword Puzzles"; "Quick and Easy Crosswords"; "Easy-Time Crosswords"; "Fast 'n' Fun Crosswords"; "Nice and Easy Crosswords" – but if you look at the answer section, you'll find many of the words excellent contenders for SAT tests. Penny Press Puzzles are fun and challenging, and they are sure to build your vocabulary a few words at a time.

2) FUN/LEARNING-ORIENTED: The Thesaurus. A thesaurus contains synonyms – words that are similar in meaning to one another. Many students use a thesaurus to locate alternate words when writing essays; others use a thesaurus for locating that "perfect" word to use in a poem or in a song. Others use their thesaurus to help find answers to crossword puzzle clues (which is my favorite use for it). Still others find a thesaurus an easy way to build up vocabulary all in itself. If you are a regular user of a thesaurus, you know that all the following words are synonyms for "shy": bashful, timid, diffident, timorous, apprehensive, demure, coy, reticent, taciturn, skittish, retiring, and reserved (among others). Such words are very popular on SATs (perhaps that's where many of the words are selected from!) and knowing them can prove a boon to your vocabulary. The thesaurus is indeed a treasure trove for SAT words!

3) LEARNING-ORIENTED: Vocabulary Word-Lists. Many books boast of such lists, and many of these lists contain highly appropriate words. However, I have found two major problems with these lists:

> 1) The words often have such lengthy definitions that it is hard to ever really learn them. One might memorize a definition one week just to forget it the next. For long-term growth, such lists meet with mixed success.
> 2) The lists are not always complete, which can lead to a false security that knowing 500 words will ensure a dramatic increase on the SAT. 100, 200 or even 500 words is not sufficient to guarantee such results.

Enclosed in this text is a helpful list of 480 words often found on the SAT, each accompanied by a simple one-word definition. Again, 480 words is not a panacea for one's vocabulary ills, but the simple definition can make it a good first step toward Verbal mastery.

Beyond the oft-encountered lists of important SAT words, there exists a book containing almost every word you might encounter on the SAT along with simple one-word definitions: *The Karelitz SAT Dictionary of One-Word Definitions*. This book, which contains 4000 SAT words along with three choices (for self-practice), has helped students raise their Verbal scores to 700 or more. It is the most comprehensive SAT vocabulary-building book on the market (and the easiest to learn from!), but it is only for those who are committed to maximizing SAT Verbal scores at a level no less than 700. It works, but it requires time and resolve.

For most students, building up test-taking strategies will result in worthwhile score-gains. But for the few who have greater aspirations, the three vocabulary-building suggestions mentioned may well prove to be the path to such success.

SENTENCE COMPLETIONS:	There are 19 SENTENCE COMPLETIONS on the SAT. They appear first in the Verbal section (before the ANALOGIES and READING portions).
BEST THING TO DO:	Work quickly and get the easy ones correct.
WORST THING TO DO:	Spend too much time on any question, especially the harder ones.
TIME:	Allow yourself ½ minute per SENTENCE COMPLETIONS question. In other words, for 10 questions allow yourself 5 minutes. Be sure you get the easy ones correct, and when you find yourself getting bogged down (hopefully it won't happen until midway through this portion) pick up the pace. Don't use up valuable minutes here or you'll regret it later, when you're on the READING portion. Skipping is also not a good idea though many students have told me they feel better simply bailing out of the section and moving on once the problems become "over their head." However, I still subscribe to the belief that you can't get lucky if you don't try. Just don't spend too much time on the final questions!

STRATEGY-APPROACH:

    1) Read the sentence.
    2) Place your own words into the blank(s).
    3) "Limited Elimination": eliminate two or three choices.
    4) Select the best answer from those that remain.
    5) Move quickly; don't waste time on the final (hard) ones.

SUGGESTIONS FOR LONG-TERM IMPROVEMENT:

    1) Practice and review your errors.
    2) Build up your vocabulary through crossword puzzles, use of a thesaurus, or word-list study.
    3) Read. This sounds like advice you've heard for years, but fact is that reading is the best long-term cure for all Verbal weaknesses. However, in today's fast-paced world reading has been kicked into the corner, forcing students to study word-lists to compensate for a lifetime of reading neglect. Sad though it may seem, that's the way it is. However, don't let that stop you from picking up a book and reading; you just might find yourself unable to put it down!

SENTENCE COMPLETIONS (*select the letter whose word(s) __best__ complete the thought of the sentence*)
(**circle your answer**)

1. Unable to convince her brother to stay, she wished him a pleasant _____.
   (A) antipathy
   (B) analysis
   (C) farewell
   (D) emotion
   (E) disposition

2. She was endowed with a _____ for spiritual _____.
   (A) fixation...powers
   (B) talent...abnormalities
   (C) gift...healing
   (D) solution...indecision
   (E) concern...resistance

3. In the spotlight, the _____ man had little difficulty _____ himself.
   (A) eloquent...defending
   (B) reticent...expressing
   (C) belligerent...pacifying
   (D) extroverted...consoling
   (E) indifferent...infuriating

4. How could such a _____ person stoop to _____ his friends?
   (A) high-minded...disparage
   (B) callous...betray
   (C) regal...extol
   (D) magnificent...ostracize
   (E) pretentious...validate

5. The effervescence of the beverage left the guest _____ and inebriated.
   (A) vigilant
   (B) giddy
   (C) malevolent
   (D) wistful
   (E) indecisive

21

6. The intractable horse let no man _____ or _____ her.
   (A) surmount...conquer
   (B) condescend...dominate
   (C) condemn...control
   (D) alienate...antagonize
   (E) tame...befriend

7. He would never admit to _____ the truth, but he was clearly not a _____ of virtue.
   (A) revealing...model
   (B) fabricating...scapegoat
   (C) stifling...reflection
   (D) obfuscating...paragon
   (E) denying...dissenter

8. Succumbing to temptation, the _____ consumed the entire ambrosial delicacy.
   (A) progenitor
   (B) heretic
   (C) anarchist
   (D) profligate
   (E) gourmand

9. The imminent _____ of the ailing corporation was a source of _____ delight for its hungry competitors.
   (A) success...unbridled
   (B) dissolution...sardonic
   (C) sale...amorous
   (D) demise...qualified
   (E) danger...unrestrained

10. The institution of marriage is an _____ bond of _____ bliss.
   (A) essential...conditional
   (B) inevitable...immutable
   (C) improbable...ecstatic
   (D) inviolable...connubial
   (E) arbitrary...sanctimonious

SENTENCE COMPLETIONS quiz problems explained

1. ·C   This problem is especially easy if you replace the blank with your own word before looking at the choices.

2. C   "Endowed" is a key word that indicates a "positive" or "good" trait being discussed. "Fixation" (**A**) fails the test, as do "abnormalities" (**B**), "indecision" (**D**) and "resistance" (**E**). **C** makes sense, too; elimination may not have even been necessary here.

3. A   "Little difficulty" is the key phrase here. In one's own words, the sentence might resemble "In the spotlight, the 'outgoing' man had little difficulty 'expressing' himself." "Belligerent" means "warlike" and "indifferent" means "not caring" — **C** and **E** are quickly eliminated. "Extroverted" fits perfectly, but "console" means to "comfort," and when one blank doesn't fit, that choice is not valid. "Eloquent," by the way, means "fluent in speech," and a person who is able to speak well would have little difficulty "defending" himself. It's not Shakespeare, but it makes sense and is the best answer.

4. A   Upon first reading of this sentence, you should be aware that the two blanks are CONTRASTIVE; more specifically, the word "stoop" indicates that the second blank is likely to be the "negative" word. So, in one's own words you might say "How could such a 'good' person stoop to 'be bad to' his friends?" Vocabulary is a problem here, but without knowing all the words there's still a good chance you can eliminate a couple of choices: how about eliminating **B** and **D** ("callous" and "pretentious" are both "negative"). If you knew that "extol" meant "praise," you could eliminate **C**. **A** is the answer: "high-minded" means "having high ideals"; "disparage" means to "belittle."

5. B   The key word is "inebriated," which means "drunk." As the sentences progress, elevated vocabulary plays a greater part. "Giddy" means "dizzy," often a result of having too much champagne (a very popular "effervescent" beverage).

6.   **E**   "Intractable" is the key word here. It is a "negative" word, so even without knowing the precise definition, you should have surmised by the prefix "in-" that, whatever the horse was, it was not good for any man. "Incense," "condemn" and "antagonize" don't seem to fit the sense of the sentence – three choices are eliminated. Vocabulary is a factor from this point on: "condescend" means to "stoop down to." **E** is the only remaining logical choice and it of course is the best answer.

7.   **D**   The final few sentence-completion problems are usually not worth the effort. If you know the words, they are fast and easy; if you don't, they are time-wasters. Eliminate what you can, pick what seems best and move on. The sentence itself is easy to translate: "He would never admit to 'hiding' the truth, but he was clearly not a 'model' of virtue." The question is which of the choices matches these words. Eliminating **A** (first blank) and **B** (second blank) is a start; It may be as close as you can get without a strong vocabulary.

8.   **E**   The sentence is easy to read, but the missing word is a herculean task to identify. We know the missing word means "big eater" or something like that (in slang, perhaps a "pig"). If you can eliminate a couple of choices, you're closer to the answer. If you know the words, this is as "easy as pie." At this stage, vocabulary is the big trump-card; there's no mystery in this section of the SAT <u>if</u> you know all the words.

9.   **B**   More vocabulary problems arise, though you might know that the words we need are "end" and "some kind of." The second blank doesn't seem to mean much; the first blank looks to hold the key to the answer. With a limited vocabulary, you have no choice but to try your hand at luck and move on. With a stronger vocabulary, you might be able to confidently eliminate choices **A, C** and **E**. Ascertaining the correct answer indeed requires knowing the remaining key words: the answer is found in the second blanks – "sardonic" means "cynically scornful" and "qualified" means "limited." ("Dissolution" and "demise" both imply "the end," by the way.) The difference between a correct answer and an educated guess is knowing more key SAT vocabulary words.

10.   **D**   It wouldn't be #10 if it weren't a vocabulary brain-teaser. At this stage, good advice is not to spend much time on the problem. Better advice is to try to quickly eliminate a choice or two. Best advice is to learn the words and get it correct! By the way, "inviolable" means "not to be broken," and "connubial" means "relating to marriage." If you know these words, this part of the SAT is a breeze! Otherwise, it's the time to bail out quickly and lick your wounds later!

Final Thought

Of the three SAT Verbal sub-sections, SENTENCE COMPLETIONS is consistently the one students perform worst on. The good news is that there aren't many of these vocabulary-oriented questions, and many of them are answerable. I have never found this section primarily responsible for a poor or excellent overall SAT score; most students score within a narrow range on it. The greatest range of scores is found on the next two Verbal portions: ANALOGIES and READING. Let's move on to see why this is so and also how you can realize 100-point gains on these two sections in as little time as one week!

SAT ANALOGIES: The Most Misunderstood Section of the SAT Verbal Test

Unlike the cut-and-dry nature of the SENTENCE COMPLETIONS, the ANALOGIES section is excitingly mysterious in the sense that the difference between scoring poorly and scoring well on this part of the test depends upon one's understanding of the directions. Those who know the little "secrets" and "tricks of the trade" can score 100 points higher than those who lack these "finer points." On the SENTENCE COMPLETIONS portion, the difference between a fair and good score is the difference between a fair and good vocabulary; on the ANALOGIES portion, such is not necessarily the case.

When I first began tutoring and then teaching SAT-preparation, I simply followed the test directions, which ask to select a pair of words that best expresses a relationship similar to that expressed in the original pair. Over time, I expanded this idea by encouraging students to form sentences to relate the words. It produced fair results, but nothing spectacular. Then I looked at it from a different perspective and directed students to use a few key words to connect the pair, but that only seemed to be a variation of the original idea.

Then, approximately six months ago, I was struck with a revelation as though a bolt out of the heavens. I awoke (yes, I was actually asleep at the time!) with this new idea, and in the months since I have used this strategic technique, ANALOGIES scores have soared! Students who got 6 out of 19 correct were suddenly getting 12 correct, a feat that is virtually impossible to do on SENTENCE COMPLETIONS. This chapter will unveil this dramatic discovery.

ANALOGIES: What They Are

ANALOGIES consist of two main words which in some way relate to one another. The object is to determine the relationship and then find a pair of words that share this relationship. For example: "SMILE: HAPPINESS." A satisfactory sentence would be "A smile expresses happiness." A possible answer could be "FROWN: SADNESS" because a frown expresses sadness. The sentence remains basically the same, though the other pair of words is substituted in place of the main pair. It is similar to a SENTENCE COMPLETIONS problem except that the "blanks" are provided and the sentence is not! This is the general rule, and by following it you can probably get the first two or three problems correct. But now let's introduce a more difficult ANALOGY: "PERSPICACIOUS: INSIGHTFUL." The difficulty in the problem is apparent: vocabulary once again is at the forefront. However, there is a strategy that can help you select a very probable answer (or, more accurately, help you eliminate unlikely choices) without knowing what the main words mean. This has been one of my most successful strategies in the past, especially because it has a high degree of success and is easy to learn and apply.

Strategic "Karelitz Approach": Think "SAME"... Think "OPPOSITE"

When you confront a word in an ANALOGY that you are not familiar with, there is little you can do to "know" the word. You might be able to break it down by prefix or root word, but usually it will do little good. However, if you can assume that the two words are the same, you can immediately look at the choices to see which might be the most logical answer. This, of course, is best achieved by eliminating a couple of choices that do not seem to be the same. It's the "limited elimination" strategy back at work. Let's try an example to see if this strategy can help you reach a correct answer even though the main words may be unfamiliar to you:

ELEEMOSYNARY: CHARITABLE::
(A) hungry: thirsty
(B) ferocious: timid
(C) thankful: wishful
(D) benevolent: kindly
(E) military: comfortable

The problem is, of course, in "eleemosynary." If this were a SENTENCE COMPLETION, you would be in a dilemma. But with the "SAME" strategy, there's a good chance you can eliminate at least one or two choices and perhaps even see the best answer materialize right before your eyes. Did you eliminate **A** and **B**? If so, you're on the right track. Does **E** make sense? If not, you've narrowed your choices and now have a fast and easy choice: It's either **C** or **D**. The answer is **D**.

This is a very helpful strategy, but there is another twist to it. Look at the following pair and you may see a second possible relationship: "INTREPID: FEARFUL." If you see a prefix that alerts you to an "opposite" ("in-" and "im-" usually mean "not"), there's a distinct possibility that the two words are antonyms (words opposite in meaning). The "OPPOSITE" strategy then comes into play. Try the following example, using your latest strategy as your plan of attack:

INCLEMENT: MILD::
(A) disturbed: angry
(B) hostile: peaceful
(C) independent: reliable
(D) commonplace: usual
(E) fragile: volatile

Again, the difficulty is due to a word in the pair: "inclement." But did you notice the prefix "in-"? It should have alerted you to the possibility that these two words might be "opposites." The first thing to do, therefore, is eliminate choices that do not fit the "opposite" relationship. **A**, **C** and **D** can be quickly crossed out. That leaves only two choices, of which **B** is the answer. Not bad for "guessing"!

I've always enjoyed the "SAME/OPPOSITE" strategy because it is easy to apply and it doesn't take up very much time. Remember this strategy when you practice with ANALOGIES: It can help you answer questions you never thought you could do!

The Latest Strategic "Karelitz Approach":
The "Missing Link" to Understanding ANALOGIES

Up to this point, I have presented you with strategies that have helped students over the past several years. They are good strategies, but I always felt that they weren't good enough.

It took one ANALOGY to open my eyes to the need for one more strategic plan of attack: DOORMAT: SHOES. What do you think is the relationship between these two words? You may know the relationship, but I have found in my classes that too many students are misled by the two words. However, after learning of this latest strategy, few if any are misled by these types of analogies ever again.

A Doormat Is Where Shoes Go On?

Did you figure this to be the relationship? If so, you are among the many who are wrong! And by misidentifying the relationship, you may very well select the wrong answer as well. I felt that if I could pinpoint the relationship between these two words, I could unlock a strategy that applies to many (perhaps half!) of SAT ANALOGIES. One night, the vision appeared: a doormat with shoes.

Why Is a Doormat?

Perhaps this sounds like Shakespeare with a headache, but that is exactly what I asked myself as I awoke. And then it dawned on me: A doormat's purpose is to clean shoes. The magic word had entered: PURPOSE. From that morning on, I began to examine SAT ANALOGIES and continually ask "Why?" For example: "PILLOW: BED." Why a pillow? What is it PURPOSE? A pillow is a <u>cushion</u> for the bed. It was then that I realized I had unearthed the "missing link" strategy, the one between the "easy" ANALOGIES and the "SAME/OPPOSITE" ANALOGIES. The "Karelitz approach" now had PURPOSE!

The Magic Word is PURPOSE!

There are several different kinds of relationships employed frequently on the SAT. For example: "WHEEL: TRUCK." A wheel is part of the truck; more specifically, its function ("purpose") is to help the truck move. Here's another example: "LETTER: ALPHABET." A letter is more than a part of the alphabet; letters comprise the alphabet. Would the following serve as a good answer: "LEAVE: TREE"? If you said "yes" you are mistaken. Leaves do not make up a tree; there are branches, too. Therefore, the key in this section is to tighten up the relationship so that only one choice remains. Rather than give a sample of each type of relationship, let's try a sample quiz of selected ANALOGIES. They incorporate a variety of relationships, but remember to always keep in mind the PURPOSE; it is a guide-word that will seldom lead you astray.

WORD PAIR:	RELATIONSHIP
1) CHISEL: CARVE	_____
2) WHALE: POD	_____
3) BAT: BASEBALL	_____
4) MENU: DINER	_____
5) HURRICANE: WIND	_____
6) SURGEON: SCALPEL	_____
7) TRACTOR: FARM	_____
8) ACTOR: STAGE	_____
9) PILLOW: BED	_____
10) BLADE: SKATE	_____
11) BEACON: GUIDE	_____
12) CAMEL: DESERT	_____
13) PATRIOTIC: COUNTRY	_____
14) CURMUDGEON: CRUSTY	_____
15) TRUNK: TREE	_____
16) HORSE: FOAL	_____
17) DUST: SNEEZE	_____
18) GROCERY: BAG	_____
19) POODLE: DOG	_____
20) BOOK: PAGES	_____

If you can get at least 15 correct, you understand the basics of ANALOGIES and will probably fare well on this part of the SAT. If you get fewer than 15 correct, pay particular attention to your errors so you do not make the same type of mistakes again.

ANSWERS: 1) a CHISEL is a <u>tool</u> used for CARVING (think "PURPOSE" here)

2) a POD is a <u>group</u> of WHALES (notice that I reversed the words for simplicity; the answer must also fit in the same order)

3) a BAT is a <u>tool</u> used (PURPOSE) to <u>hit</u> a BASEBALL (or, a BAT is a <u>tool</u> used in the sport of BASEBALL)

4) a MENU is a <u>list</u> (think PURPOSE!) that <u>offers selections</u> in a DINER (or, a MENU is a <u>list</u> that <u>offers selections</u> for a DINER, a person who dines)

5) a HURRICANE is a <u>big/powerful/destructive</u> WIND

6) a SCALPEL is a <u>tool</u> used by a SURGEON (also, thinking PURPOSE, it <u>cuts</u>)

7) a TRACTOR is a piece of <u>machinery</u> that is used on a FARM

8) an ACTOR <u>performs on</u> a STAGE

9) (think PURPOSE here!) a PILLOW helps <u>cushion</u> a person on a BED

10) a BLADE is <u>a part of</u> a SKATE and (think PURPOSE!) it helps the skate move

11) (use your STRATEGY here!) a BEACON GUIDES (in other words, "<u>SAME</u>")

12) a CAMEL <u>lives</u> on a DESERT (be sure to distinguish between "natural" and "artificial" environment; the answer would <u>not</u> be "FISH: AQUARIUM")

13) PATRIOTIC is a <u>good feeling</u> for one's COUNTRY

14) (use your STRATEGY here!) "<u>SAME</u>" (a CURMUDGEON is CRUSTY)

15) a TRUNK is <u>part of</u> the TREE (think PURPOSE!) that helps <u>support</u> it

16) a FOAL is a <u>baby</u> horse

17) DUST <u>causes</u> a person to SNEEZE (cause: effect)

18) GROCERIES are <u>kept/transported</u> in a BAG

19) a POODLE is a <u>type</u> of DOG

20) a BOOK <u>consists</u> of PAGES (similar to TREE: LEAVES)

Did you notice some of the more subtle relationships, such as PATRIOTIC: COUNTRY? Oftentimes you will need to determine whether a word is a "feeling," a "characteristic," a "sense" (etc.) before you can tie in its PURPOSE-relationship with the other word. Here's another distinction that you may find helpful in eliminating wrong choices:

SHACKLE: MOVEMENT::
(A) anchor: ship
(B) gag: speech

Which of these is the correct answer? You may have established that a SHACKLE <u>prevents/stops</u> MOVEMENT, but this may not be enough. Here's another "gimmick"-strategy: Determine whether the word is tangible ("able to be touched"). Can you touch "movement"? Can you touch a "ship"? The answer is therefore clearly **B**; you can't touch "speech." In order to have made **A** correct, what would the second word in the main pair have to be? (This is a good way to "check" your answers; see if the main pair works when you look first at the ANSWERS you have selected.) In this problem, the main pair would have to be SHACKLE: LEG or SHACKLE: BODY. Determining the tangible nature of a word can help you get the ANALOGY correct.

In the following list, simply describe generally what it is. This practice may prove to really help you make sense out of ANALOGIES. And once you feel comfortable doing them, you'll be fast and you'll score well!

1)	CANOE	_____
2)	TRUTH	_____
3)	MESSAGE	_____
4)	HELMET	_____
5)	ODOR	_____
6)	COPYRIGHT	_____
7)	GLASS	_____
8)	MUMBLE	_____
9)	PROLOGUE	_____
10)	ARGUMENT	_____
11)	ANGER	_____
12)	MANSION	_____
13)	SAVORY	_____
14)	BICYCLE	_____
15)	INJURY	_____
16)	LIBRARY	_____
17)	COUNTERFEIT	_____
18)	IGNORANCE	_____
19)	BOREDOM	_____
20)	RUDDER	_____

If you can get 15 or more correct, ANALOGIES are no longer a problem!

ANSWERS: 1) <u>transportation</u>

2) <u>intangible "thing"</u> which would include possible related words as LOVE, FACT, BELIEF, UNDERSTANDING, etc.

3) <u>something that contains information</u> (it might be tangible or it might not, depending upon whether the message is a letter or simply the information contained)

4) <u>something that protects</u> (and is worn)

5) <u>something released and able to be perceived</u> (such as the related word FRAGRANCE)

6) <u>something that protects</u> (but it is <u>not</u> tangible as "helmet" is)

7) <u>a container</u> or (if interpreted differently) <u>material that something is made of</u>

8) <u>indistinct</u> action (related word: SCRIBBLE)

9) <u>something that comes before something else</u> (related words: PREFACE/INTRODUCTION)

10) <u>bad/hostile condition/situation</u> (not tangible)

11) <u>strong emotion</u>

12) <u>large</u> house (key word: <u>large</u>)

13) <u>good to the senses</u> (related words: DELIGHTFUL/BEAUTIFUL/APPEALING)

14) <u>transportation</u>

15) <u>bad condition</u> or <u>result of something bad</u>

16) <u>place that contains/stores</u> things (related words: BANK/SUPERMARKET)

17) <u>misleading condition/thing</u>

18) <u>bad/inept state/condition</u>

19) <u>bad/dissatisfied condition/state of being</u>

20) <u>tangible thing that steers</u>

You needn't get the exact description as long as you were close with regard to its "nature" (thing/condition/feeling/etc.) and its PURPOSE (transportation/protection, etc.). Once you see ANALOGIES from this PURPOSEFUL perspective, you will find all of them easy to follow and easy to select a logical answer for. The "SAME/OPPOSITES" strategy will apply when you don't know a word, though you may still be able to look at the word you do know and determine the relationship. The following example demonstrates this approach:

SKULK: MOVE

Even if you don't know what "skulk" means, you might be able to eliminate choices by recognizing that "move" is a "body action." If the second-word choices were

(A) :smile
(B) :watch
(C) :withdraw
(D) :analyze
(E) :shake

which ones would you eliminate? If you narrowed the choices down to **C** and **E**, you've done your homework. The others do not fit the general description of "body movement." At this stage you might need to guess, but the odds are much better than if you had not looked at the second word with this new perspective.

The "Ship List"

Not all ANALOGIES work out so easily, even with our strategic approaches. There are always a handful that tend to baffle the best of ANALOGIES experts. I have produced a sample selection of such pairs, called the "ship list." They do not fall into the "SAME/OPPOSITE" pattern but yet are challenging enough to defy constructing a simple sentence. The "SKULK: MOVE" approach is oftentimes all you can do to eliminate a choice or two and make a daring guess. By the way, these are usually found at the end of the ANALOGIES section, so you know they are not meant to be easy; few students get them correct. In this list, I haven't even listed possible choices, so you are really on your own! See if you can get 10 or more correct!

WORD PAIR:	RELATIONSHIP:
1) BELL: PEAL	_____
2) TOOTH: COMB	_____
3) RUNNER: SLED	_____
4) CODICIL: WILL	_____
5) AVIARY: FLY	_____
6) ANEMOMETER: WIND	_____
7) QUIVER: ARROW	_____
8) TUNNEL: MINE	_____
9) FOUNDER: SHIP	_____
10) SLAG: METAL	_____
11) NIP: MATURE	_____
12) STEM: TIDE	_____
13) GOBLET: GLASS	_____
14) ISLAND: ARCHIPELAGO	_____
15) FACE: CARICATURE	_____
16) LEGEND: MAP	_____
17) DRAKE: DUCK	_____
18) CHAFF: WHEAT	_____
19) COVEN: WITCHES	_____
20) SHIP: LIST	_____

ANSWERS:
1) a PEAL is the <u>sound</u> of a BELL
2) a TOOTH is <u>part</u> of a COMB
3) a RUNNER is the <u>blade</u> on the SLED (PURPOSE: it helps the sled move)
4) a CODICIL is something <u>added</u> to a WILL
5) an AVIARY is an <u>enclosed area</u> where things inside FLY (related words: CAGE/AQUARIUM)
6) an ANEMOMETER <u>measures</u> the velocity of WIND (it's a "tool")
7) a QUIVER is a case that <u>contains/holds</u> ARROWS
8) a TUNNEL is a <u>passageway</u> in a MINE
9) when a SHIP FOUNDERS, it sinks (by the way, there is no relationship between a "founder" – noun – and a "ship")
10) SLAG is the <u>unusable/worthless part</u> of METAL after it has been processed
11) when something is NIPPED, it <u>prevents it</u> from becoming MATURE
12) to STEM is to <u>hold back</u> the TIDE
13) a GOBLET is a <u>fancy</u> GLASS
14) an ARCHIPELAGO is a <u>group</u> of ISLANDS
15) a CARICATURE is a <u>comical exaggeration</u> of a FACE
16) a LEGEND is a part of the MAP that <u>explains</u> the symbols
17) a DRAKE is a <u>male</u> DUCK
18) CHAFF is the <u>discarded/useless part</u> of the WHEAT
19) a COVEN is an <u>assembly/group</u> of WITCHES
20) When a SHIP LISTS, it is <u>tilting</u> (by the way there is no relationship between a "list" – noun – and a "ship")

The good news about these "wolves in sheep's clothing" is that such ANALOGIES are infrequent on the SAT and are usually reserved for the final one or two problems. The more-common ANALOGIES can be successfully solved by our battery of strategic approaches: the "make a sentence" approach; the "SAME/OPPOSITE" strategy; and the "PURPOSE" strategy (the "missing link" strategy!). Once you practice and review sample SAT ANALOGIES, you will soon find yourself becoming amazingly proficient on this section. Best of all, it does not require vocabulary-building; however, knowing the words is undeniably the panacea for all SAT Verbal ills.

ANALOGIES:	There are 19 ANALOGIES on the SAT. They appear after the SENTENCE COMPLETIONS.
BEST THING TO DO:	Work quickly and use "limited elimination."
WORST THINGS TO DO:	1) Spend too much time on any question. 2) Skip.
TIME:	Allow yourself ½ minute per ANALOGIES question. In other words, for 10 ANALOGIES allow yourself 5 minutes.
STRATEGY-APPROACH:	1) Look at the two main words and determine the relationship between them. (Think PURPOSE as well as other key connectors such as TOOL/MACHINERY/TRANSPORTATION/EMOTION/CHARACTERISTIC...) 2) "Limited Elimination": eliminate two or three choices. If the words are difficult, think "SAME" or "OPPOSITE" and eliminate unlikely choices. 3) Select the best answer from those that remain.

Whatever you do on this section, do it quickly. The next section is the most critical on the SAT Verbal Test; you don't want to have to rush on the READING portion!

SUGGESTIONS FOR LONG-TERM IMPROVEMENT:
  1) Practice and review your errors.
  2) Build up your vocabulary through crossword puzzles, use of a thesaurus, or word-list study.

Sample quiz

ANALOGIES (*select the letter whose words <u>best</u> express a relationship similar to that expressed by the words in capital letters*) **(circle your answer)**

1. SURGEON: OPERATE::
   (A) TEACHER: EVALUATE
   (B) MECHANIC: MODIFY
   (C) CALCULATOR: SIMPLIFY
   (D) CURATOR: REMEDY
   (E) ADVISER: COUNSEL

2. GIGANTIC: SIZE::
   (A) EXPENSIVE: AFFORDABILITY
   (B) MONSTROUS: APPEARANCE
   (C) INCREDIBLE: BELIEF
   (D) COLOSSAL: STRENGTH
   (E) INFINITESIMAL: MAGNITUDE

3. POTHOLE: AUTOMOBILE::
   (A) TIME LAPSE: MEMORY
   (B) COLD WAVE: SLEIGH
   (C) TIDAL WAVE: SURFBOARD
   (D) STUMBLING BLOCK: CONVOY
   (E) AIR POCKET: AIRPLANE

4. FLAG: PATRIOTISM::
   (A) PENNANT: COMRADERY
   (B) HEART: LOVE
   (C) WISH: HOPEFULNESS
   (D) PROMISE: DEVOTION
   (E) AWARD: DEFEATISM

5. SEISMOLOGIST: EARTHQUAKE::
   (A) BOTANIST: PLANT
   (B) BICYCLIST: RACE
   (C) METEOROLOGIST: METEOR
   (D) OCULIST: GLASS
   (E) DENTIST: TEETH

6. SINNER: REDEEM::
   (A) FUGITIVE: FREE
   (B) PREACHER: CONVERT
   (C) CAPTIVE: LIBERATE
   (D) GLUTTON: REDUCE
   (E) REFORMIST: CONDEMN

7. DERANGED: LUNATIC::
   (A) INTREPID: COWARD
   (B) EXPERT: VETERAN
   (C) ENTHUSIAST: LAGGARD
   (D) WISE: SAGE
   (E) BEFUDDLED: CONTESTANT

8. DECLIVITY: ASCEND::
   (A) AMITY: BOLSTER
   (B) DETERIORATION: PROGRESS
   (C) SHORTAGE: EXPAND
   (D) DELIGHT: ACCUMULATE
   (E) DEBACLE: ASPIRE

9. COORDINATED: MALADROIT::
   (A) LITHE: WOODEN
   (B) INTOXICATED: UNSTEADY
   (C) PROLIFIC: PRODUCTIVE
   (D) CONCISE: VAGUE
   (E) SPLENDID: GLORIOUS

10. ELUCIDATE: CLARITY::
    (A) BAFFLE: RESOLUTION
    (B) HALLUCINATE: OBSCURITY
    (C) JEOPARDIZE: PERIL
    (D) INCRIMINATE: IMPRISONMENT
    (E) DECELERATE: INACTIVITY

ANALOGIES quiz problems explained

1. **E** A SURGEON is a <u>person</u> whose professional job it is to OPERATE. An ADVISER is a <u>person</u> whose professional job it is to COUNSEL

2. **D** Something GIGANTIC is <u>very great</u> in SIZE; something COLOSSAL is <u>very great</u> in STRENGTH: (Something MONSTROUS is very great in SIZE, not APPEARANCE; INFINITESIMAL means very <u>small</u>, not <u>great</u>)

3. **E** A POTHOLE is something that an AUTOMOBILE may run into that negatively affects the quality of the ride. An AIR POCKET is something that an AIRPLANE may run into that negatively affects the quality of the ride. (An AUTOMOBILE is a specific/individual means of transportation; a MEMORY and CONVOY are not).

4. **B** A FLAG is a <u>symbol</u> that <u>reflects</u> PATRIOTISM. A HEART is a <u>symbol</u> that <u>reflects</u> LOVE.

5. **A** A SEISMOLOGIST is a <u>professional person</u> who <u>studies</u> EARTHQUAKES. A BOTANIST is a <u>professional person</u> who <u>studies</u> PLANTS. (A METEOROLOGIST studies WEATHER; an OCULIST is an EYE DOCTOR; a DENTIST does not study TEETH – he cleans/fixes them)

6. **C** The key word here is REDEEM, which means to SET FREE. When a SINNER is REDEEMED, he is no longer a sinner – he has been released from his sins. A CAPTIVE is no longer a captive after he has been LIBERATED. (A FUGITIVE is a <u>wanted man</u>; he is already FREE but not free from his crime.)

7. **D** The "SAME"/"OPPOSITE" strategy-approach works well here. These two words are basically the SAME. The next step is to ELIMINATE choices that are not the same. **A** and **C** are opposites; **E** is totally unrelated... **B** and **D** remain. With a strong vocabulary (gained by doing crossword puzzles!), you would know that "sage" is a "wise man." A "veteran" is an "experienced person," though not necessarily an "expert."

8. **B** The "SAME"/"OPPOSITE" strategy-approach works well here, too. But a light bulb should flash, warning you that these words are not the same; in fact, they are OPPOSITES. All you need to do is eliminate a couple of the choice-pairs that are NOT opposites and the answer is within reach. The pair of words in **A** are not related, as is the case with those in **C** and **D**. A "debacle" is a "complete collapse"; to "aspire" is to "hope to become" (the two words are thus not related). The answer is easy <u>if</u> you know the words; otherwise, it's strategic elimination and lucky guesswork.

9. **A** The "SAME"/"OPPOSITE" strategy-approach is once again highly effective. These two words are OPPOSITE ("MAL-" might have given you a clue; it means "bad"). The easiest pairs to eliminate are those in **B** and **E**. If you know the definition of "prolific," you will be able to eliminate **C** ("prolific" means "highly productive"). The difficulty is in choosing between the final pair of choices. The opposite of "concise" is "verbose" or "long-winded"; the opposite of "vague" is "precise" or "clear." In this manner of reverse-comparison, you can tell that CONCISE and VAGUE are not actually opposites. "Lithe," by the way, means "graceful"; "wooden" means "awkward and ungraceful." (Did you also notice that both pairs related to body-movement?!)

10. **C** This is the hardest analogy, which is to be expected when it is the final problem of the section. The "SAME"/"OPPOSITE" strategy-approach works well once again; these two words are basically SYNONYMS. The problem is that all the choices seem to fit the same general relationship. The specific similarity is that when something is ELUCIDATED, it <u>brings about a condition</u> of CLARITY. When something is JEOPARDIZED, it <u>brings about a condition</u> of PERIL (to JEOPARDIZE something is to put it in danger; PERIL is "danger"). Working backwards, we can eliminate the other choices: to BAFFLE is to CONFUSE, not bring to RESOLUTION ("solution"); to HALLUCINATE is to see unreal visions – OBSCURITY simply means "haziness" or "lack of clarity"; to INCRIMINATE is to accuse someone of a crime – it does not necessarily imply that the person is being or will be IMPRISONED; to DECELERATE is to "slow down" – INACTIVITY means "not active" or "not moving at all."

The ANALOGIES portion is the most strategically significant sub-section of the SAT Verbal, though not for the reason you might perhaps think. A major goal in this chapter has been to help you master ANALOGIES; but more importantly, I hope you have learned how to solve the problems <u>quickly</u>. If you can get most of the problems correct, your overall score will undoubtedly benefit; but if you can do so quickly, you will be "ahead of the clock" and in the "driver's seat" for the all-important READING section.

- MYTH #7: SENTENCE COMPLETIONS and ANALOGIES usually determine the SAT Verbal Score.

  - FACT: It is the SAT READING section that will most likely determine your SAT Verbal success.

What you gain in the next chapter will indeed most likely leave its mark on your overall SAT Verbal score. Now do you know what kind of test the SAT primarily is?

It's time to move on to the bread-and-butter of the SAT Verbal. If you've got the time, I've got the strategy!

SAT READING: The "Make-It-Or-Break-It" Part of the SAT Verbal

> • MYTH #8: The SAT is primarily a test of reading ability.
>
> > • FACT: The SAT is _not_ primarily a test of reading ability.

By the end of this chapter, you will at last know what the SAT is really all about. Although the SAT includes a vast amount of reading – on the Math section as well – it is not primarily a reading test. In fact, even the READING portion of the Verbal is not primarily a test of reading ability.

The Primary Goal on the READING Section

What is your primary goal on the READING section? Ponder this question for a few moments. Is it to READ? Do you think it matters how well you read or enjoy the passage, or even if you enjoyed it at all? Do the SAT test-makers want you to explain what you read or how you liked the passage? Of course not! The SAT contains reading passages followed by a certain number of questions, many of which have little to do with the main points of the essays. In fact, I would say that nearly half of the questions do not relate at all to key parts of the passages; they are focused instead on specific lines and phrases as well as less-significant portions of the essays. If I were to grade the test-makers on their focus on the main points of the passages, I doubt I would even give them a C-. But that's not their goal; instead, they simply want to know if you can answer questions based on the passages. No one said you need to fully comprehend a passage; no one even said you have to read it. But if you don't answer the questions correctly, then you are failing in your primary goal: to maximize your SAT score.

> • MYTH #9: The goal of the READING section is to read and understand the passage.
>
> > • FACT: The goal of the READING section is to answer the questions correctly.

Reading and understanding may help you reach your main goal, but reading a passage is not the ultimate goal of the SAT READING.

> • MYTH: The best approach to scoring well on the SAT READING is to select the correct ("best") answer.

I know you must really be confused now! Most SAT programs and SAT instructors believe that the best approach is to look for the correct answer. They are wrong, and by the end of this chapter you will know more than the SAT professionals do about the READING section! (This MYTH will be revisited and demystified later in the chapter.)

SAT READING: A General Analysis

Before I open your eyes to the strategic "Karelitz approach" to SAT READING, let's quickly review this portion. SAT READING comes after the ANALOGIES and comprises the final part of each Verbal section. There may be one or two passages, or there may be a double-reading passage (two passages concerning the same topic). Each is followed by anywhere from 5 to 13 multiple-choice questions asking anything from the main idea to the definition of a word as it has been used in the passage. The questions are very focused and may be more concerned with a minute detail than the passage as a whole. Reading the passage slowly and carefully will not ensure that you will be able to answer the questions correctly; you will more than likely need to refer back to the passage to answer almost every question. The main concern is to answer the questions, not necessarily understand the essay.

> • MYTH #10: Some questions require deeper interpretation of the essay.

The instructions ask you to answer the questions based on what is <u>stated</u> or <u>implied</u>, and many people over the years have interpreted "implied" as "something that is not stated" and therefore must be deduced. This is simply not true. "Implied" simply means that it is "stated indirectly." For example, you do not need to interpret "The daytime sky was dark and cloudy" to realize that what has been implied is that the weather was not very pleasant. In simpler words, "implied" means "stated in other words."

> • FACT: The SAT READING questions are all based on what is in the passage.

This is why the adage "Stick with your first choice" applies so well on the SAT Reading; second thoughts usually result from "interpreting" something that has <u>not</u> been stated (or implied) in the passage. If the choice isn't mentioned in the passage, that choice is not the correct answer! This is not a test of interpretation; it is a test of recognition. Your job is to discover which choice is the best <u>based on what the passage says</u>.

> • MYTH #11: You can answer the READING questions without reading the passage.

Even though your primary objective is to get as many questions correct as possible on the READING section, fact is that you will not do well if you don't have a good idea what the passage is about. In an experiment, I tried to answer SAT READING questions without reading the passage, but despite my advanced test-taking skills and strategies, the results proved without a doubt that even a skilled test-taker cannot answer questions that are based on a passage without first reading it. I selected answers that seemed the most logical, but I soon discovered that SAT READING answers are not based on logic; they are based on what is in the passage.

> • FACT: Reading the passage may not be the primary goal, but it is an essential step toward reaching the goal of maximizing your SAT score.

> • MYTH #12: If you don't know an answer, pick C.

All carefully-prepared tests are made with a mathematical regularity; that is, in a test of five choices, each choice will appear approximately 20% of the time. In other words, in the long run every letter (**A, B, C, D,** and **E**) will appear the same number of times.

> • FACT: Guessing **C** gives you the same odds as guessing **A** or **E** or **B** or **D**.

Sometimes there will be five **A** answers in a row, or maybe three **A** answers followed by two **E** answers: there is simply no predictable pattern. Therefore, there is no reliable strategy regarding guessing. If you find yourself relying on this type of strategy, you might as well bring your lucky four-leaf clover and wear your lucky ring. They'll all yield the same results. I prefer a more dependable plan of attack.

> • MYTH #13: You should read/look over the questions before reading the passage.

Let's quickly dispel this myth. As mentioned earlier, the types of questions on the SAT require you to go back even after having read the passage.

> • FACT: Looking at the questions beforehand does nothing but waste time and confuse.

Strategic 4-Step "Karelitz Approach" to Maximize Your READING Score

1) Read the italics (at the beginning of each passage). This usually-short introduction will give you an idea as to the general subject of the passage and may even shed some light on the mood of the essay. For example:

"The following is an excerpt from a poet's nostalgic recollection of her youth prior to emigrating to the United States."

From this short introduction we can glean valuable information about the author, the nature of the essay, and the nostalgic mood enveloping the thoughts presented. Without this information, you may find yourself uncertain of the nature of the passage, and the result may well be three or four avoidable wrong answers.

2) Read the passage quickly. Don't skim but instead read with the purpose of trying to understand the main idea. Don't get bogged down by facts and names you can't pronounce. If the reading is predominately fact-oriented (as often with Science passages), skip the "boring" parts and quickly move on to the next key point. (Chances are that any questions regarding technical data will be accompanied by line-number references anyway, so don't worry about it now!) When you have finished the first read-through, you should have a good general idea what the essay is about and what the mood/tone is. The sample essay introduced above was obviously "nostalgic," but others are not so clearly spelled out in the italics. The first read-through should give you all the information you need to progress to Step #3.

Speed-Reading: A Priceless Skill

I want to take a moment to address a problem many students have: reading. Do you find yourself reading the same line twice? Do you find yourself slowing down and getting stuck on one word? Do you find yourself losing concentration as you read? Do you find yourself falling asleep when you read an SAT passage? I have a remedy that has proven to be nearly 100% successful. The answer is in your finger!

Why are there lines on the side and in the middle of the road? Well, what would happen if you drove along a road that had no lines on either side? Most drivers would probably find themselves straying off the road or drifting into another lane. The lines serve to keep your eyes focused on the road; drivers don't look directly at the lines but instead use the lines as markers to keep them focused straight ahead.

In this same way, your finger can keep your eyes focused and moving ahead as you read the passage. Simply use your index finger to "scan" each line; your eyes will follow and read right behind the moving finger. You will find that you no longer repeat lines or find yourself slowing down. In addition, the guiding finger lessens the strain on the eyes because it keeps you focused on the line. It is a marvelous reading strategy because it embodies the basic tenets of speed reading in an effortless, simple manner. What can be easier than using your finger to help you read!

By the way, if you read something that appears to be worth remembering, take a moment to underline or circle it. Then if you find yourself wanting to return to that portion, you will have easy access to it. In addition, the temporary pause will allow you to better review the point; it may help in the total comprehension of the essay. Remember, you are encouraged to write on the test booklet; it will simply be discarded after the test is scored. With the "finger-strategy" and the "underline strategy," you now have test-proven techniques that will help you make this first read-through a very successful (and speedy) one!

3)   Answer the <u>easy</u> questions. Unlike the SENTENCE COMPLETIONS and ANALOGIES, the questions in the READING section do <u>not</u> progress from "easy" to "hard." Instead. they generally develop as the passage develops: from "beginning" to "end." Therefore, you need to determine which questions are the easiest to answer. Practice will help you become experienced in this step. But for starters, remember that questions referring to "line numbers" are usually easy to answer, as are questions that ask about the "main idea." The "harder" questions usually involve longer references ("lines 24-45 refer to...") or more provocative questions ("If the author were to follow the advice of his critics, which of the following would he most likely choose to do?".

• MYTH #14: Questions with line numbers are the easiest questions.

This is not necessarily true.

• FACT: Questions with line numbers are the easiest to answer, but not necessarily the easiest to get correct.

This is an important distinction. In this step, your goal is to answer the questions that do not require a deeper reading or the use of much time. Occasionally, a question that is easy to answer is a difficult one that most people get wrong. However, this does not change the fact that the question was easy to identify and answer in a minimum of time.

In Step #3, the primary goal is to get as many questions out of the way so that Step #4 will be easier to manage.

• MYTH #15: If a question refers to "line 15," the answer will be found on line 15.

This is as far from the truth as could be imagined. The line-reference simply indicates where the word or phrase in question is located.

> • FACT: The answer to a question referring to a line number will either be found
> before or after the line; it will rarely be found in the line itself!

For example:

"In line 26 – 'The hikers viewed the obstacle as but another demonstration of the power of Mother Nature' – what does 'obstacle' refer to?"

In this hypothetical question, you can be sure the "obstacle" is not clearly specified in the sentence. Maybe it was mentioned in the previous sentence or maybe in the previous paragraph. Or maybe it will be explained in the next sentence or the next paragraph. The point is, it is not answered in line 26. The same is true in the following example:

"In line 18, the word 'fugitive' means..." You can be sure that the answer will not be found in line 18, and the definition of the word may not be what you think it is; it all depends on how the word has been used in the passage.

This type of question can probably be answered with a quick review of surrounding lines and is obviously one you will want to answer during Step #3. Whether or not the question itself is an easy, medium or hard one is not our concern. If it can be answered without a deeper reading, do so in Step #3.

> • MYTH #16: The best approach to scoring well on the SAT READING is to select
> the correct ("best") answer.

This MYTH (which I mentioned briefly in the beginning of the Chapter) is greatly responsible for substandard SAT READING scores. Even the instructions tell you to select the best answer. To me, this misleading advice is setting you up to fail!

> • FACT: On the SAT READING, select the WRONG ANSWERS!

That's right. Look for all the wrong answers...and eliminate them. Every single READING question should be handled in this way. Look for any part of the question that makes it false, then eliminate it as a possible answer. When you have eliminated two or three choices, then select the best (correct) answer from what remains. You will experience a dramatic improvement in your number of correct answers. The more often you use the "limited elimination" strategy, the better your score will be!

4) Having answered the "easy" questions, all that remains are the more involved (and often the most difficult) questions. Having looked at – and answered many of – the questions, you know what information you still need to glean to answer these remaining questions. With this in mind, read through the passage again but with the understanding that you only want to answer the remaining questions; your goal is not to simply reread the passage in depth. Because each section is timed and the READING is the final part of the Verbal section, you will know how much time you have left to answer these remaining questions. In addition, since the remaining questions are most likely the more difficult ones, you needn't feel worried if you feel that you are "guessing" a bit more than usual. Eliminate two or three choices and select what you think is the best answer from the remaining choices. (You can feel comfortable knowing that in Step #3 you answered the bulk of the questions.) If time is very short, you may not wish to reread the passage but instead simply try to answer what remains to the best of your ability. The goal in Step #4 is to use your remaining time to answer the remaining questions and thereby maximize your potential READING score.

The ANSWER to the Original Question: The SAT is primarily a _____ test.

I have waited until the end of the Verbal discussion to unveil the answer to the question originally posed on page 6. The answer is actually the key behind maximizing one's score on the Verbal and Math sections of the SAT.

What is the one element that is most crucial in allowing you to do well on the READING section? (Remember, the READING section is the most important part of the SAT Verbal score; what you do on this section will invariably determine your level of success on the Verbal test.) Imagine a football or basketball game in which your team is behind by twenty points with only a couple of minutes remaining. Compare this to a scene in which you have a READING passage left on the Verbal section with only a couple of minutes to complete it. In the game, your best-laid plans won't produce twenty points in the remaining two minutes; there simply isn't enough time remaining to put any plan of attack into effect. On the SAT, the four-step reading strategy and the finger-strategy can't help you anymore because there simply isn't enough time remaining to implement the strategies.

> • FACT/ANSWER: The SAT is primarily a <u>time-management</u> test.

If you can work quickly through the SENTENCE COMPLETIONS and ANALOGIES, you will have enough time to utilize all the strategies on the most critical section of all: READING. The more time you have for the all-important READING section, the better your score will be. Now you know the real truth behind maximizing your SAT score. The key element is TIME!

Let's Review

READING:	There are 40 READING questions on the SAT, involving four or five total reading passages. They appear after the ANALOGIES (except in the 15-minute section, in which all questions are READING questions).

BEST THING TO DO: Allow yourself enough <u>time</u> to put the strategies ("finger-strategy"/"4-Step" strategy using "limited elimination") into full service.

WORST THING TO DO: Leave yourself too little time to utilize the strategic "Karelitz approach."

TIME: Use it all! If you finish early, go back and look over your READING answers. Do not put your head down to rest; you may wake up to find that the test has ended and everybody has gone home!

STRATEGY-APPROACH: 1) Read the italics.
2) Read the passage quickly.
3) Answer the easy questions.
4) Review the passage to answer the remaining (hard) questions.

SUGGESTIONS FOR LONG-TERM IMPROVEMENT:
1) Practice taking sample SAT Verbal sections to be sure your time-management is under control. In addition, you can practice the "finger-strategy" as well as the 4-Step "Karelitz approach."
2) Develop your concentration skills through very effective verbal puzzles:

CROSSWORD PUZZLES – excellent not only for vocabulary-building but also for building concentration skills.

LOGIC PROBLEMS – excellent for problem-solving and thinking, but most importantly for building concentration skills.

CRYPTOGRAMS and ANACROSTICS – verbal puzzlers that require concentration.

CODE WORDS – simple but challenging verbal teasers that require concentration.

SUM TOTALS – arithmetic crossword-puzzle-like teasers that build problem-solving and concentration proficiency.

*NOTICE THE COMMON DENOMINATOR:
<u>building concentration skills will improve READING skills!</u>*

The puzzles described above are all contained in PENNY PRESS VARIETY GAMES magazines available at your favorite supermarket.

The following two passages concern the similarities between the lives and assassinations of two American Presidents. Passage I reflects upon events common to both; Passage II is a reaction to the phenomenon discussed in Passage I.

PASSAGE I

line

Striking parallels exist between the lives of Abraham Lincoln and John F. Kennedy, two American Presidents whose terms were each cut tragically short by an assassin's bullet. Though politics usually shares nothing with parapsychology, the uncanny similarity of events surrounding the lives of these two men might well bolster one's belief in the supernatural.

5   Abraham Lincoln, elected in 1860 as the 16th President of the United States, was an active proponent of Civil Rights, issuing in 1863 the Emancipation Proclamation which liberated the slaves in the southern states. Later in 1863, he delivered the Gettysburg Address which reaffirmed the principles of equality laid down a hundred years earlier by the nation's founding fathers.

John F. Kennedy, elected in 1960 as the 35th President of the United States, was also a social activist
10   whose ambitious support of Civil Rights was evidenced by his innovative New Frontier program and his establishment of the Peace Corps to assist those oppressed abroad.

Of greater curiosity are the events surrounding each great man's death. Both occurred during public events, and each involved a shooting. Prior to the murders, each President was advised not to appear at the site. Mr. Lincoln was so advised by his personal secretary, named Kennedy; Mr. Kennedy was
15   given the precaution by his secretary, Mrs. Lincoln.

The lives of the assassins themselves also share eerie similarities. John Wilkes Booth, Lincoln's attacker, was born in 1839; Lee Harvey Oswald, Booth's counterpart, was born in 1939. In addition, neither of these two men ever went to trial for murder: each was himself shot and killed shortly thereafter.

20   Even the aftermaths of the tragic deaths contain spine-shilling similarities. Andrew Johnson, born in 1808, assumed the Presidency upon Lincoln's death; Lyndon Johnson, born in 1908, assumed the Presidency upon Kennedy's death. Both Johnsons were Southern Democrats who had previously served in the U.S. Senate. Both served as Presidents during politically turbulent times, and both declined to run for office in a subsequent election – Andrew Johnson in 1869, Lyndon Johnson in
25   1968.

A popular expression states that "Religion and politics don't mix"; however, an examination of the facts and circumstances surrounding the lives and deaths of both Presidents seems to suggest that otherworldly forces may at times interact with mundane ones. America can only look with apprehension to the year 2060, when yet another statesman will rise to what may well be another ill-
30   fated Presidency.

Perhaps more than ever before, religion and politics may need to mix; this future period of uncertainty could well be one in which a nation's prayers may best serve to ward off the spell of tragic events begun two centuries earlier.

line

The so-called similarity between the presidencies of Lincoln and Kennedy reflects the temperament
35   of a nation that all too easily subscribes to mystical and superstitiously fallacious logic. A further
analysis of these two historical figures will expose this folly.

Para-historians have noted that "Lincoln" and "Kennedy" each contains seven letters, of which "N"
is the only one in the alphabet common to both. In fact, the letter "N" is used twice in each name.
However, we can further analyze alphabetical correlations between these two beloved leaders to such
40   a degree that everything, even the obvious, begins to seem eerily coincidental. The first letters of
"Lincoln" and "Kennedy," L and K, are both consonants as well as adjoining letters in the alphabet;
more strikingly, one letter in each name is used exactly three times: "A" in Abraham Lincoln"; "N"
in John Kennedy." In an even more stupefying display of alphabetical and numerical prestidigitation,
each President's full name averages exactly seven letters: Abraham Lincoln – two words, fourteen
45   letters; John Fitzgerald Kennedy – three words, twenty-one letters. The magic numbers three
(mentioned earlier) and seven add up to 10, the number of letters in JFK's middle name, Fitzgerald.
The letter "J", amazingly, is also the tenth letter of the alphabet.

Through a warped mirror of reflection, the assassinations of these two great figures also bear a
striking resemblance. Each man was sitting down as he was shot (and lying down, thereafter) and
50   each was shot by a bullet fired from a gun (though Kennedy was shot at several times with a rifle).
The name of each assassin – John Wilkes Booth and Lee Harvey Oswald – consists of three words
(Kennedy's predator could therefore have been Lyndon Baines Johnson, but that's another theory)
and each outlived the man he shot (a correlation that might include other greats such as Julius Caesar
and Mahatma Gandhi).

55   With so many fascinating parallels so easily uncovered, it is no wonder that a gullible public might
interpret the events as preordained. But I submit that, as with television psychics and stock market
prognosticators, correlations are a product of reflection, not prediction: everything is clearer with 20-
20 hindsight. For example, it was reported that both Presidents were dissuaded from attending the
ill-fated public events, but so too are we all faced with daily decisions: should we take the bus or car
60   to work; should we eat eggs or cereal for breakfast; should we go through the yellow traffic light or
not? Were we to regard every decision as momentous and potentially life-threatening, would it not
behoove us to simply stay home and not venture out at all? With such apprehension, who would ever
wish to dare anything new, least of all aspire to such a tragically lofty position as to one day become
President of the United States?

65   There comes a time in everyone's life when rabbit's feet and lucky socks need to be replaced with
personal responsibility and commitment. For those wishing to become President in the year 2060,
let no tales of witchcraft or divine voodoo derail your ambitions. In a land easily mesmerized by
occult nonsense and groundless phobias, it is all too easy for a person to be led down a path of fear-
induced anxiety. Two great Presidents gave their lives in defiance of such narrow-mindedness; we
70   should laud such rebel spirit and refute overtly offensive attempts by so-called mystics to manipulate
us through misguided, purposeless superstition.

READING (*select the letter of the choice that <u>best</u> answers the question, based on what is <u>stated</u> or <u>implied</u> in the two passages*) (circle your answer)

1. Passage **I** is primarily concerned with
    (A) philosophy
    (B) democratic ideals
    (C) famous people
    (D) a tragic situation
    (E) similarities of historical events

2. In line 8, "fathers" most closely means
    (A) heads of households
    (B) political leaders
    (C) architects
    (D) teachers
    (E) natives

3. In line 17, "counterpart" refers to
    (A) a President
    (B) a similar event
    (C) a Vice-President
    (D) an assassin
    (E) an exception

4. Why does the author of Passage **I** look upon the year 2060 with apprehension?
    (A) It may be the year an ill-starred person assumes office.
    (B) It will climax a half century of societal depravity.
    (C) It represents an arbitrary year in an uncertain future.
    (D) It may be the year a tragic event takes place.
    (E) It may mark the beginning of years of political upheaval.

5. Which of the following words from Passage **I** is the target of mockery in Passage **II**?
    (A) parapsychology (line 3)
    (B) equality (line 8)
    (C) curiosity (line 12)
    (D) religion (line 31)
    (E) politics (line 2)

6. In which paragraph does Passage **II** begin to resort to outlandish and ludicrous correlations?
    (A) paragraph one (beginning on line 34)
    (B) paragraph two (beginning on line 37)
    (C) paragraph three (beginning on line 48)
    (D) paragraph four (beginning on line 55)
    (E) paragraph five (beginning on line 65)

52

7. What information is revealed in Passage **II** that is not mentioned in Passage **I**?
    I.   The year of the assassinations
    II. The names of the assassins
    III. A President's middle name

  (A)   I only
  (B)   I and II
  (C)   II only
  (D)   II and III
  (E)   III only

8. The topic being discussed in both passages most closely concerns
  (A)   the hereafter
  (B)   religion
  (C)   historical biography
  (D)   the occult
  (E)   politics

9. In what manner does "stupefying" (Passage **II**, line 43) help convey the author's overall tone?
  (A)   The word implies both "amazement" and "dullness."
  (B)   The word is purposely misused.
  (C)   It has no "N"s in it, accentuating the meaninglessness of the argument.
  (D)   Its use conveys that the public is "stupid."
  (E)   It effectively exhibits the author's elitist attitude.

10. In which of the following did the two Presidents <u>not</u> share a curious similarity?
    I.   the names of their secretaries
    II. the years of their birth
    III. the letters in their names

  (A)   I only
  (B)   I and II
  (C)   II only
  (D)   II and III
  (E)   III only

11. What word would best describe how the author of Passage **II** considers the author of Passage **I**?
  (A)   evil
  (B)   timid
  (C)   confused
  (D)   misled
  (E)   demented

12. What is the primary purpose for the parenthetical comments in Passage **II**?
    (A) They add critical information.
    (B) They present the author's personal opinions.
    (C) They ridicule the points being made.
    (D) They question the reliability of the data.
    (E) They bolster the arguments presented.

13. Which pair of words used in Passage **I** and **II**, respectively, best summarizes each author's attitude toward the subject matter that has been conveyed to the public?
    (A) uncanny; gullible
    (B) eerie; mesmerized
    (C) spine-chilling; warped
    (D) ambitious; offensive
    (E) turbulent; purposeless

14. Which of the following do the authors each make reference to in the passages?
    I.   Civil Rights
    II. a saying
    III. the future

    (A) I only
    (B) I and II
    (C) I and III
    (D) II and III
    (E) I, II and III

15. Both authors would most likely agree that
    (A) numbers can be fascinating
    (B) the future is unpredictable
    (C) both Lincoln and Kennedy were destined to be shot
    (D) religion and politics don't mix
    (E) superstition is a powerful social force

READING quiz problems explained

1. **E** When a question asks what a passage is "primarily" about, you need to identify what is <u>generally</u> being discussed. Some of the choices may be discussed in the passage, but the question is focused on the overall idea that runs throughout the passage. Passage **I** is primarily concerned with the similarities between the two Presidents, especially the assassinations of both. The focus of the argument is on the events surrounding the assassination – what happened before, during and after. **A** and **B** are not related to the essay. **D** is not the main focus of the analysis in Passage **I**, and although the passage does discuss two famous people (re: choice **C**), the main focus is on the events that have made the lives and deaths of both eerily similar in nature.

2. **C** The READING strategy-approach emphasizes the need to read the passage(s) quickly and then answer the "easy" questions first, before going back to re-read and answer the remaining ones. This is one of those "easy to answer" questions, though the answer is not as easy to get correct. The answer, as we know, will likely not be found on the indicated line, but instead before or after, in a related discussion. In this instance, the word is rather well-contained within the same sentence (lines 7-9); therefore, with a basic idea of the historical nature of the essay, one will be immediately aware that the use of "fathers" is very specific. **A** and **D** do not fit the context and can be immediately eliminated. The question now becomes "What is a founding 'father'?" Our limited-elimination strategy has narrowed the answer to three choices, two if you were able to eliminate **E**. Now it's just a matter of determining which of the remaining choices best fits the context of the word in question.

3, **D** This is a very easy question: it is easy to answer and easy to get correct. The reference-word is actually in lines 16-17. Take advantage of these simple line-number questions; they are quick and easy to answer.

4. **A** Unlike the previous two questions, this one is not easy to answer and therefore should be deferred until a closer reading has taken place. According to lines 29-30, 2060 is the year another statesman will assume the Presidency. **B** and **C** can quickly be eliminated, leaving us with three choices to look at. A closer reading of the paragraph will reveal that not only is this the year the President is elected to office, but this may be the same person who will soon be assassinated. The year does not represent the "beginning of years of political upheaval" and is not the year that any assassination is expected to take place. It simply marks the start of the term for a President who may eventually become the victim of an assassination.

5. **A** At first glance, this looks to be an easy question. But further inspection will show that each choice must be carefully considered in comparison with a counterpart word mocking it in Passage **II**. "Mockery" implies making fun of through ridicule, so the word must be the target of some verbal attack. "Equality" is not a word that is mocked in Passage **II**, nor is "religion" or "politics." "Curiosity" could be a word worthy of mockery, but there is no instance where the author of Passage **II** picks up on the word to mock it. "Parapsychology,"

however, is mocked on line 37; the author uses his own "para-" word "para-historians," whom he shortly thereafter exposes as nothing but charlatans displaying "alphabetical and numerical prestidigitation." There is a direct association between the two "para-" words, one used seriously in Passage **I**, the other word used mockingly in Passage **II**.

6. **B** This type of question is usually easy to answer. It is based on the essay's construction as much as its content. The key is to identify where the "outlandish and ludicrous correlations" begin. Paragraph Three is definitely a mockery of the "coincidental" theory, thereby eliminating the later paragraphs referred to in choices **D** and **E**. Paragraph One does not show specific correlations. The question is whether Paragraph Two contains any silly comparisons, which indeed it does.

7. **E** Whenever a question lists possible choices which are incorporated into the answer-choices, you can be sure this question requires a more thorough reading of the passage(s). You will need to examine each passage to see whether the points were discussed, then compare to see which of the points are contained within the choices. These are usually easy questions to answer correctly, though not necessarily questions that can be answered quickly. From a second and closer reading, you will notice that the years mentioned in Passage **I** include each President's year of birth, the year each was elected to office, the year each assassin was born, and the year the succeeding President was born. No mention is made in Passage **I** of the year of the assassination itself. (Passage **II** lists no year other than 2060, which may be an even quicker way to eliminate **A** and **B** as choices.) Both essays mention the names of the assassins, eliminating **C** and **D** as possibilities. A deeper reading (which may not be necessary if four choices have already been eliminated!) will reveal that John Kennedy's middle name, "Fitzgerald," is mentioned in Passage **II**; reviewing Passage **I**, you will notice there is no mention of the full middle name, simply the initial "F."

8. **D** As with question 1, this question is general and therefore quick and easy to answer. The key is to eliminate what is <u>not</u> the most general issue being discussed. "The hereafter" refers to "heaven," which is not the topic of discussion; nor do the essays concern themselves with "politics" but rather the lives of two political leaders. "Religion" is never mentioned except as an afterthought in the expression "Religion and politics don't mix." Thus, **A**, **B** and **E** have been eliminated. The decision is between whether the essays are primarily concerned with "biography" or "the occult." Your first instinct will probably tell you that it is about those eerie coincidences in the two men's lives. Trust your instincts; they usually will guide you to conclusions based on the reading itself, not on second-thought interpretations. The essays are historical in nature and are biographical in content, but the main topic is in the eerie similarities found common in both Presidents' lives. ("Similarities" is mentioned in the introductory italics, by the way.) In other words, the focus is on the "occult," those mystical forces beyond the normal world that have similarly affected the two historical figures.

9. **A** At first review, this question looks easy to answer, but upon closer inspection you will see that it combines two very difficult elements: interpretation and vocabulary. You need to determine "What is the purpose for the author using 'stupefying'? as well as "What does 'stupefying' mean?" Fortunately, even without a clue as to the true meaning of the word in question you can eliminate irrelevant or silly choices such as **C** and **E**. The question remains as to the definition of "stupefying" and whether the author has used the word correctly or incorrectly (and, if incorrectly, whether he has done so on purpose). Those with a well-grounded vocabulary know that "stupefying" has two definitions, one of which implies filling a person with "amazement" and the other which more closely means "dulling a person's senses," as alcohol might do. The word's double-entendre serves to better illustrate the author's sarcastic tone, on one hand suggesting that the number/letter correlations are "amazing" while at the same time implying that the public is so unaware as to be "dull" to the truth as if in a drunken stupor. The question is intriguing and simple-looking, but the answer is very difficult to get correct.

10. **C** Similar to question 7, this question requires a second reading; answering it immediately will use up more time than you care to give up after the first quick reading. But when you do eventually return in the remaining minutes to answer this question, you will find it straightforward and therefore quite easy to answer correctly. Because the question is not asking you to compare the passages, you need only read to locate if the two elements mentioned share a curious similarity. Passage **I** clearly mentions the curious similarity in the Presidents' secretaries' names, and both passages discuss the letter-formations in the names (Passage **II**, however, has done so in mocking fashion). But nowhere is there mention of the year of each President's birth, though the years of the birth of their successors has been stated. Elimination is once again the best strategic approach to determining the best answer.

11. **D** This type of question is easy to answer once you've gotten a general idea what the passages are about. It may not be an easy question to get correct, but it is an easy one to answer quickly. Passage **II** has made fun of Passage **I**; the author of Passage **II** thus considers the other author as either a bit silly or simply ill-advised. The first author is not looked upon as "evil" or "timid," which eliminates **A** and **B**. You must now select from "confused," "misled" and "demented." Choice **E** means "crazy," a description that does not accurately reflect the tone of the second passage toward the author of Passage **I**. "Confused" implies that the first author does not know what he is saying, yet the second author does not question the facts at all. Rather, he feels the earlier author is stating facts that, though well-intended and acceptable at face-value, are misleading in assuming that these coincidences imply some greater forces are at work. He therefore looks upon the earlier author as a person misled by randomly-selected though admittedly-coincidental and curious information.

12. **C** At first glance, this question looks very easy to answer. In one sense, it is; but the answer may be deceptively complex. In order to answer this question correctly, the parenthetical comments must be interpreted as the author intended: as sarcasm. Then the words will begin to make more sense; they simply bring out the silliness of the original points. For example, it may be curious that both people were shot while sitting, but it seems obvious that after they were shot they would be lying down. The parenthetical remark makes the original observation trivial and seeks to expose it as just as absurd as the more tongue-in-cheek observation. Thus, the question can be answered quickly and easily but only with a proper understanding of the author's tone – which may require a second and more thorough reading.

13. **C** As with the last question, this one seems easy to answer but again requires a deeper understanding of the tone of each passage. A second, more thorough reading is helpful to better grasp the nature of each passage and therefore answer questions such as this one. The author of the first passage is very serious about the subject; the author of the second passage is equally as serious but in exposing the errors in logic of the earlier "occult" theory. Elimination is the key approach here: look for any word that does not answer the question. For example, the first author has not viewed the events as "turbulent," nor has the second author viewed the subject matter as "mesmerizing." You needn't worry about the other half of each choice: **B** and **E** are eliminated. Looking at the remaining three choices, you might feel hesitant about "ambitious" as a word summarizing the first author's attitude about the theory, and indeed you'd be correct in eliminating **D** as well. **A** sounds correct – "uncanny" surely fits the first author's perspective regarding the coincidental nature of the events surrounding both Presidents. However, though "gullible" describes how the second author views the public, it does not reflect how he views the subject matter. Instead, he calls the theory of coincidences a distorted theory which has been manipulated to deceive the public into believing such superstitions. In other words, the subject matter has been "warped" to bolster the "occult" theory. (By the way, "spine-chilling," "uncanny" and "eerie" each could be used to describe the first author's attitude toward the subject matter; it was the second word of the pair that eventually determined the best answer.)

14. **D** We have seen this type of problem twice before. By now you know this may be easy to answer, though not after a quick first-reading. This question requires a second reading and then time to sort through the possible choices. Passage I discusses the Civil Rights issue, but Passage II never mentions it. We can therefore eliminate **A, B, C** and **E**. That was quick! This question simply worked itself out without my deeper analysis needed. But for the curious, both passages do reflect on the future, each referring to the year 2060. The saying "Religion and politics don't mix" is mentioned in Passage I; and though never directly referred to as a saying, lines 57-58 in Passage II do allude to one when saying that "everything is clearer with 20-20 hindsight." This could have been a difficult answer had it not been that the elimination of **I** settled the issue all by itself!

15. **E** This final question seems quite innocuous; it simply requires a general understanding of the tone of each passage. But the comparative nature of the question is deceivingly difficult. Elimination of obviously-wrong answers is imperative. **B** and **C** can be quickly eliminated: the author of Passage I would not agree that the future is unpredictable and the author of Passage II would not subscribe to any theory that predestiny plays a significant role in past or future events. **A** sounds feasible, but "fascinating" does not seem to be the appropriate adjective for either author – "eerie" would more closely fit as a description from the first author; "deceiving" would be a more appropriate adjective given by the second. **D** applies well to the author of the first passage, but the second passage's author offers no comment regarding whether religion and politics are related. Instead, he simply implies that occult theories and superstition have no logical validity and do not relate (except by sheer coincidence) with real events. Both authors would agree that superstition plays a major role in influencing society; the difference is that the second author does not believe the public should be so gullible.

Final Thought

+

A Final Word on the Verbal Section of the SAT

The degree of success one has on the READING portion of the SAT usually correlates closely with the degree of success on the SAT Verbal as a whole. If you pace yourself to allow ample time to devote to this portion of the test, you will likely realize an amazing increase in your Verbal score.

The SAT is time-constrained. Everything you do must be within the prescribed time limit. (This, you will soon discover, is equally true on the Math section.) Getting the easy questions correct will usually ensure a score of 500 or more. If you can get most of the READING questions correct (for example, 30 out of 40 correct), you have almost certainly locked in at least a 600. But the key behind maximizing your success on the SAT Verbal is not the strategies themselves; it is in managing your time so you can actualize your strategic plan of attack. With appropriate time available, you can put the "Karelitz approach" into effect to boost your SAT Verbal score 100, 200, even 300 points within a month. Many of my students have accomplished this feat, and it has not been due to luck or magic. You can do it too, if you pace yourself with disciplined time-management.

It is now time to begin to analyze the SAT Math test, a test that is not a math test at all!

The **SAT MATH** Section (The Ideal Test for Those Who Hate Math): An Overview

The SAT contains three types of Math problems:
MULTIPLE CHOICE
QUANTITATIVE COMPARISONS (column-comparisons)
STUDENT-PRODUCED ANSWERS ("grid-ins")

- MYTH #17: The SAT Math section is a test of mathematics skills.

- FACT: The SAT Math section is a test of time-management.

All mathematics problems on the SAT are very basic; they do not test any skills beyond Geometry and Algebra I. Many of the problems involve fractions and percents, others are even simpler in construction. The key to maximizing your SAT Math score is to work slowly and carefully so that you can answer each problem correctly. Unlike in the Verbal section, Math problems do not seek the "best" answer; they demand the "correct" one. Your primary goal on each problem you do is to therefore understand the question fully so you can answer it correctly.

- MYTH #18: You should not skip any SAT Math problems.

- FACT: You should work slowly and carefully and not expect to do every Math problem on the test.

On the Verbal section, the key is to eliminate and select the "best" answer from what remains; on Math, the key is to work out the problem in your test booklet and determine the "correct" answer, then look at the choices to see which one matches your answer. The emphasis here is on accuracy, not speed.

- MYTH #19: Each problem on the SAT Math section is worth the same.

- FACT: The problems on the first half of the SAT Math section are worth more than the others.

As in the Verbal section, the first few Math problems are the most important because they are the easiest and therefore the ones you are most likely to get correct. Your primary goal on the Math section should be to get as many problems correct as possible and not spend your time wastefully on ones you probably won't get correct. Unlike in the Verbal section, where your time-management responsibility is to move quickly and use all remaining minutes on the READING section, in the Math section your time-management responsibility is to work slowly and carefully on the easy (first) problems, answer as many as you can correctly and don't worry about doing the final few hard problems. The overall strategic approach on the SAT Math section is therefore quite different from the Verbal approach.

> • MYTH #20: The SAT Verbal favors students with Verbal skills; the SAT Math favors students with Mathematical skills.

> • FACT: Both sections favor students with good Verbal skills.

Before we begin analyzing the Math portion of the SAT, it is important to recognize that most students find this section difficult because of the way the questions are worded. Once the problem is explained to them, students usually can solve the problem without much effort. In fact, the SAT Math section is more accurately a "reasoning test," a test that purports to measure reasoning and problem-solving proficiency. The test-makers do not claim it to be a test of mathematical knowledge. (The SAT II Subject Test in Math – which many colleges also require – is moreso a test of mathematical comprehension; it is not, however, part of the SAT I, the test this book is addressing.) The following SAT Math problem illustrates this problem-solving focus:

Two book shelves stand side by side, each with eleven compartments. One compartment can contain one book only. As a book is stored, it automatically goes onto the left shelf. As each book is added, each previous book is moved over one compartment to the right. Once the left shelf is filled, each subsequent book placed onto the shelf results in a book from the left shelf going onto the right shelf. For example, if three books are added to a full left shelf, then three books on its right side will automatically move to the right shelf's leftmost side. Twenty-two books, of course, will result in both shelves being filled.

Question: If the left shelf is full and the right shelf is empty, where will the middle book on the left shelf wind up after six more books are added?
(A)   In the last compartment of the left shelf
(B)   In the first compartment of the right shelf
(C)   In the third compartment of the right shelf
(D)   In the middle compartment of the right shelf
(E)   In the second-to-last compartment of the left shelf

Admittedly, this is a very long problem to read, but it is a problem a Second-grader could solve. The difficulty is in comprehending what is being asked; it is therefore a "Second-grade" math problem dressed up in a "high school" verbal format. On an SAT, fewer than half those confronting this problem would probably answer it correctly; many would simply skip the problem and use the time more wisely elsewhere. As demonstrated by this example, the difficulty with SAT Math problems is usually not in the math but the verbal element. If you can concentrate on the problem and take the time to understand what it is asking, you will most likely solve it correctly, no matter how weak you may be in high school math. The answer, by the way, is **B**.

- MYTH #21: The SAT Math requires knowledge of formulas.

> - FACT: The SAT Math section provides you with whatever basic formulas you might need, though most of the test does not concern itself with any formulas whatsoever.

Once you practice solving SAT Math problems, you will quickly discover that they are not math problems at all. They do not focus on testing you on your ability to solve complex algebraic equations or graph linear functions, and they certainly do not ask for you to know your Geometry Theorems and Corollaries. Instead, the bulk of the questions involve common sense and basic arithmetic applications. In fact, many 9th Graders score higher than 11th and 12th Graders on this section because the material is geared more to their math level. Indeed, this is not a high school math test at all!

The #1 Cause of Low SAT Math Scores

You might think that poor time-management is the primary cause for low Math scores, but there is a more pervasive enemy that undermines what would otherwise be very satisfactory scores: careless errors. There are two specific underlying causes for such avoidable mistakes: rushing and not reading the question carefully. They can both be easily remedied by proceeding slowly and carefully. In essence, carelessness is related to poor time-management, but it is also a result of poor concentration. Therefore, to maximize your SAT Math score all you need to remember is to take your time, do the problems you understand and stay focused on each problem so you don't become the victim of carelessness. This applies to all the different problem-types: the multiple choice questions, the quantitative comparison problems, and the student-produced-answer section. The game-plan approach remains unchanged on all portions. If you stick to this mind-set, you will ensure at least a 500 on the SAT Math section.

THE S.A.T. DOESN'T GO BEYOND ALGEBRA AND BASIC GEOMETRY. COMPARED TO WHAT THE A.C.T. REQUIRES, YOU CAN HARDLY EVEN CALL THE S.A.T. A MATH TEST!

YOU'RE RIGHT! IF YOU READ EACH QUESTION CAREFULLY AND FOLLOW DIRECTIONS, YOU'LL BE ABLE TO ANSWER JUST ABOUT ANY S.A.T. QUESTION CORRECTLY! THE KEY IS TO READ CAREFULLY, AND NOT WORRY ABOUT KNOWING FORMULAS AND DRAWING FANCY CHARTS!

IF IT'S SO EASY, THEN WHY DO PEOPLE PANIC AND THINK THE S.A.T. MATH IS SO HARD?

PERHAPS BECAUSE THEY'RE RUSHING AND NOT TAKING THE TIME TO LOOK AT EACH PROBLEM USING A "COMMON SENSE" APPROACH. IT REALLY IS A VERY EASY MATH TEST, EVEN FOR 9TH AND 10TH GRADERS!

A Quick Overview of the SAT Math Section

The SAT contains of 60 math questions: 35 are multiple choice questions, 15 are quantitative comparisons, and 10 are "student-produced answers" (which are similar to multiple choice problems except that you must solve the problem yourself without the aid of five possible choices). The easier problems are at the beginning, the harder (oftentimes, the more-confusing and time-consuming) problems are toward the end. Although illustrations occasionally accompany a problem, your task in solving the question will often require additional work such as setting up a simple equation, drawing your own illustration, or doing whatever else the problem might require. If you are proficient in math, you will find the problems fast and easy to solve; for you, completing the entire test is certainly not out of the question. If you are slow or weak in math, you will find that you can achieve quite satisfying scores by spending your time on the earlier (easier) problems; don't skip any of the easy problems and try not to venture into the "land of confusion" (the harder problems). If you practice your strategic approach beforehand, you will find the SAT Math score to be everything you have hoped for. Maximizing this section of the SAT does not require vocabulary or any special math skills; it simply requires careful time-management. Use your time wisely and don't make careless errors.

```
•   FACT:  Practice Makes Perfect
```

No place is this more true than on the SAT Math section. Once you feel comfortable trying all the problems and once you can achieve a score of 650, you are much closer to an 800 than you might think. The difference between a 650 and 800 is simply avoiding careless mistakes. If you have achieved a 650 already, you simply need to practice and fine-tune your approach. But for the rest of us who would be tickled pink to reach 500 or 550, the next sections are especially for you!

SAT Math MULTIPLE CHOICE Problems

Similar to the Verbal SENTENCE COMPLETION section, each Math MULTIPLE CHOICE problem first requires a careful reading before it is solved. Once you have read and understood what the problem is asking, solving it should be an easy task. The key is to concentrate and analyze the problem. Through practice, you will soon discover that there is a minimum of algebra and geometry in the test, with more emphasis placed instead on practical application and problem-solving.

> • MYTH #22: Every problem on the SAT Math section should be answered.

This may be true for those who are fast and proficient in such problems, but for those who seek a mid-range score, following such advice could prove harmful. In fact, over the years I have found that the best and worst scores share one thing in common: all the test problems are answered. The obvious distinction is that the first group gets the answers correct; the second group doesn't. More specifically, those who know what they are doing have adequate time to solve all the problems; those who are weak in problem-solving tend to rush and make careless errors because they feel they need to answer all the questions, even the last (hardest) ones.

> • FACT: On the SAT Math section, solve as many problems as you can,
> especially the easy ones. Work slowly and carefully and do not expect to finish
> the test unless you are very strong in this section.

Rushing to Finish: A Grave Misconception

Too many SAT test-takers have the mistaken impression that they've got to answer every problem on the test. Perhaps it's a product of school-tests, which are timed to fit within a scheduled period and are scored on the basis of the total number of problems correctly answered, with no penalty for wrong answers. The SAT Math section does not follow the same rules, however. With the 1/4-point penalty and a scoring system that allows a student to score quite well without having to get 80% of the problems correct, the test encourages you to progress at your own pace. For the student who feels compelled to complete the test, the result is often careless, avoidable errors: mistakes in addition or subtraction; solving the problem but answering the wrong question; filling in the wrong bubble on the answer sheet; and other related errors. These are not "knowledge" errors; these are silly, mindless errors that can be easily avoided by working slowly and carefully. Whether you are an excellent or weak student in math, you will find that rushing causes mistakes unrelated to math. That's why I have recently begun to describe the SAT Math test as "a Verbal test with numbers"; there is more reading and comprehension than math in most SAT Math problems. If you take the time to approach each problem with this in mind, you will find yourself making fewer careless mistakes. The big difference is that, unlike on its Verbal counterpart, here you can spend ample time on a problem; you do not need to worry about a READING section at the end!

A 200-Point Gain...in seconds!

Those who attempt to hurriedly answer every Math problem usually commit several careless errors along the way. These same students are also likely to find themselves simply guessing on the final (hardest) problems as well. Such a haphazard approach usually produces scores in the 370-440 range. If this is your score-range, you are probably following this misconceived strategy-approach. A better approach is to do two-thirds of the test (skipping the final one-third completely), working slowly to minimize careless errors. Such a game-plan yields scores in the range of 570-620, nearly 200 points higher than before. It's amazing how quickly a Math score can increase; such phenomenal increases on Verbal can only happen with practice and vocabulary-strengthening.

Once you gain confidence in your game-plan, stick with it and you will always attain the same success. Stray from it and you will probably find your score reverting to its earlier, disappointing numbers. The only way to see how well you can do is to practice and score sample SAT Math tests. As you practice more, you will probably find yourself progressively improving on your time-management, resulting in an increase in the number of problems you are able to solve correctly.

Because MULTIPLE CHOICE problems comprise well over 50% of the Math test, it is important to establish your game-plan on these problems before venturing out to improve on the other sub-sections (COLUMN COMPARISONS and GRID-INS). If you can properly manage your time here, the other math problems will pose no major time-threat to you. I am always delighted when students tell me the MULTIPLE CHOICE problems are getting easier for them to do, because then I know they are in the driver's seat and in full control of a dramatic score-improvement. Put simply, once you master MULTIPLE CHOICE problems you have mastered all the SAT Math problems; COLUMN COMPARISONS and GRID-INS are nothing more than MULTIPLE CHOICE problems presented in a slightly different format! Master the MULTIPLE CHOICE portion and you've got the upper hand on the entire Math test. But remember that the key to maximizing your Math score is to channel your time and effort where it will generate the best results; your main focus should be to answer the easiest problems with the goal of completing two-thirds of the test with as little carelessness and rushing as humanly possible. Do more only if your goal is to score over 650; however, be realistic with your potential or you may find yourself back on the careless approach.

Strategic Four-Step Problem-Solving "Karelitz Approach":
SAT Math MULTIPLE CHOICE Problems

1) Read the problem carefully. Determine what is being asked.

2) Determine how to go about solving the problem. Take your time on this step. Rushing here will only leave you confused or else divert your attention toward answering a question that is not being asked. If you can identify what steps need to be taken to solve the problem, you are most likely going to get it correct. If, on the other hand, you do not understand what to do, don't waste time – move on to the next problem. After all, you can always come back to it if you have time later on.

3) Solve the problem, using whatever approach you feel is appropriate. Many times, you may need to draw a picture or graph to better visualize the problem. At other times, the choices may help you determine the correct answer. The important thing to remember is to always show your work. The more problems you work out, the more problems you will get correct.

4) Before bubbling in your answer, take a moment to review the question to be sure that's what you are answering. Most careless errors are rooted either in erroneous calculation or in not answering the question being asked. These are very avoidable errors; be careful you don't fall victim to them!

The following are typical SAT Math MULTIPLE CHOICE problems. Follow the "Karelitz approach" game-plan: If you don't understand a problem, go on to the next one (return later if it is worthwhile); answer the ones you feel are easy and work slowly/carefully. This may be a timed test, but when it comes to Math you've got all the time you need to complete whatever you can. There is absolutely no governing rule that says you should finish the test.

When you are done, look over your mistakes to see which were careless and avoidable. The SAT Math test is amazingly repetitive; therefore, once you catch your mistakes you are likely not to fall for the same type of error in the future. Try your best and you'll see your score (and your confidence) zoom!

(circle your answer)

1. $18 - 5 + 3 \times 0 =$
   - (A)   0
   - (B)   10
   - (C)   13
   - (D)   16
   - (E)   18

2. How many positive integers between 21 and 50 are divisible by 6?
   - (A)   8
   - (B)   4
   - (C)   3
   - (D)   6
   - (E)   5

3. The product of two prime numbers can be which of the following?
   - I.   an even number
   - II.   an odd number
   - III. a prime number

   - (A)   I only
   - (B)   I and II
   - (C)   II only
   - (D)   II and III
   - (E)   I, II and III

4. The perimeter of a rectangle is 22 and its length is 2 more than twice the width. The area of the rectangle is
   - (A)   24
   - (B)   11
   - (C)   44
   - (D)   16
   - (E)   28

5. If **X** is a member of the set {2, 4, 6, 8} and **Y** is a member of the set {1, 3, 5, 7}, how many different values are there for **X** + **Y**?
   (A)   4
   (B)   7
   (C)   9
   (D)   12
   (E)   16

Questions 6 and 7 refer to the following operation:
   $\underline{a} = 2a - 3$
   $\underline{\underline{a}} = 3a - 2$

6. What is the value of $\underline{2} + \underline{\underline{3}}$?
   (A)   22
   (B)   20
   (C)   13
   (D)   8
   (E)   5

---

7. Which of the following is equivalent to $\underline{4} + 2(\underline{\underline{3}})$?
   (A) $\underline{9} + \underline{\underline{3}}$
   (B) $\underline{18} - \underline{\underline{8}}$
   (C) $\underline{5} + \underline{\underline{3}}$
   (D) $\underline{16} - \underline{4}$
   (E) $\underline{5} + \underline{\underline{5}}$

---

8. **A** represents the set of prime integers between 11 and 19. **B** represents the set of composite integers between 7 and 13. What is the maximum value of **A** - **B**?
   (A)   4
   (B)   6
   (C)   9
   (D)   10
   (E)   12

---

9. If $y = -1$, then $-y^6 =$
   (A)   -6
   (B)   -1
   (C)   0
   (D)   1
   (E)   6

10. If $3^{2x-2} = 9^{12}$, then $x =$

   (A)   7
   (B)   8.5
   (C)   19
   (D)   21
   (E)   22

---

11. Tom bowled four games and averaged 155. What does he need to average in the next two games for an overall average of 170?

   (A)   160
   (B)   180
   (C)   185
   (D)   190
   (E)   200

$$2x - 3y + 2z = 4$$
$$5z + 4y - 3x = 7$$
$$2x - 7z - y = 9$$

12. Given the equations above, what is the value of $2x$?

   (A)   40
   (B)   20
   (C)   14
   (D)   6
   (E)   2

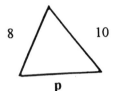

8   10

p

note: <u>figure not drawn to scale</u>

13. If **p** is an integer, what is the least possible value for **p**?
  (A)   10
  (B)   8
  (C)   6
  (D)   3
  (E)   2

---

14. If it takes **r** ounces to fill **s** bottles of perfume, how many bottles can be filled with **t** pounds of the fragrant liquid?
  (A) $\dfrac{16st}{r}$

  (B) $\dfrac{rst}{16}$

  (C) $\dfrac{16r}{st}$

  (D)   16t - s/r
  (E) $\dfrac{16t}{rs}$

---

15. In Bob's Ice Cream Parlor, sundaes are served with three scoops of ice cream. If his menu includes chocolate, strawberry, vanilla, and mint, how many different types of ice cream sundaes can be made? (note: A sundae may contain more than one scoop of the same flavor; the order of the ice cream flavors does not affect the type of sundae.)
  (A)   12
  (B)   15
  (C)   18
  (D)   19
  (E)   20

Did you have enough time to do the ones you knew? You probably did, and what's more you probably got them correct. You may have also realized that a calculator helps only on occasion; at other times it is easier to simply work out the problem in your test booklet. I have found that students perform poorly when they rely too heavily on their calculators. Those who score best are those who understand the problem and use their calculators only when computation is needed. In general, SAT Math problems can be solved without the use of a calculator. A calculator can be helpful, but it can also impede the problem-solving process necessary to adequately comprehend and correctly answer the questions.

MULTIPLE CHOICE quiz problems explained

1. **C** This problem requires proper order of operations. Multiply and divide first, then go back and add and subtract. The final step should read: $18 - 5 + 0 = 13$.

2. **E** As with almost all mathematics problems, this one should be worked out to avoid any potential careless error. The integers between 21 and 50 that are divisible by 6 are: 24, 30, 36, 42 and 48.

3. **B** The best way to approach this type of problem is to select a couple of prime numbers and multiply them. For example, $7 \times 7 = \underline{49}$ which is odd. Therefore, **II** is possible, which eliminates **A**. 2 is a prime number, and $2 \times 7 = \underline{14}$ which is an even number. Thus, **I** is also possible. We can now eliminate **C** and **D**. The only question remaining is whether any of our products ($\underline{49}$ and $\underline{14}$) are prime numbers. They are not: **E** is therefore also eliminated.

4. **A** In many instances, a picture will prove to be quite helpful. This is one of those situations. Draw a rectangle and label the sides x and $2x + 2$. With a drawing, it's easier to see that the perimeter is

$$2 (x + 2x + 2) = 22$$
$$6x + 4 = 22$$
$$6x = 18$$
$$x = 3.$$

Replacing the value for each variable yields dimensions of 3 x 8. The area is then easily found by multiplying the two numbers.

5. **B** Work this problem out carefully and you will get it correct. Select one number from one set and add it to each of the numbers of the other set. Then take the next number from the first set and repeat this process. You will find your results to be:

3, 5, 7, 9
   5, 7, 9, 11
      7, 9, 11, 13
         9, 11, 13, 15

Always be sure to double-check that you have answered the question being asked before moving on to the next problem. In this problem, there are 16 values, but only 7 <u>different</u> values.

6. **D** Questions 6 and 7 are much easier than they might at first appear to be. They simply contain made-up operations governed by a set of instructions; your job is to follow instructions to solve the problem. In this specific problem, the answer is found by doing the following:

$[2(2) - 3] + [3(3) - 2]$
$= (4 - 3) + (9 - 2)$
$= 1 + 7$
$= 8$

7. **D** The second problem of a "made-up" set is usually more time-consuming, though not usually very difficult. In this problem, you need to evaluate each choice until you come up with a result that matches the original problem. To save time, once you have a match you needn't work any further. However, as time is not the critical factor in this section (getting the correct answer is more important than being time-conscious) don't worry if you are forced to work out all the choices. It's worth the time if you can get it correct.

$\underline{4 + 2(\underline{3})} =$
$[2(4) - 3] + 2 \times [3(3) - 2]$
$= 5 + (2 \times 7)$
$= 19$

(A) $= [2(9) - 3] + [3(3) - 2] = 15 + 7 = 22$
(B) $= [2(18) - 3] - [3(8) - 2] = 33 - 22 = 11$
(C) $= [2(5) - 3] + [3(3) - 2] = 7 + 7 = 14$
(D) $= [2(16) - 3] - [3(4) - 2] = 29 - 10 = 19$
(E) $= [2(5) - 3] + [3(5) - 2] = 7 + 13 = 20$

8. **C** To find a minimum or maximum value, you need to select the largest value of one and the smallest value of the other (when the operation involves subtraction) or the smallest or largest values of each (when the operation involves addition). In this problem, you need to determine the greatest value of **A** and the smallest value of **B** that satisfies the question. In this problem, **A** must be a prime integer between 11 and 19, and **B** must be a composite (non-prime) integer between 7 and 13. the solution-sets are:

   A: {13, 17}
   B: {8, 9, 10, 12}

The answer can now be easily obtained by determining which numbers to choose to get the maximum value. It's quite easy: 17 - 8. The answer is obvious once you've set the problem up correctly. For more practice on this type of problem, try the Skill-Building Prep Quiz on page 82.

9. **B** This is an easy-looking problem, but be careful or you will get **D** as your answer. Substituting -1 for y, you will have $-(-1)^6$. $(-1)^6 = 1$, but don't forget that the problem wants $-(1)$, which of course is -1.

10. **C** This problem requires basic knowledge of exponents. The key here is know where to start: simplifying 9^{12} to a common base is the best place. $9^{12} = (3^3)^{12} = 3^{36}$; therefore substituting 3^{36} into our original problem, you have $3^{2n-2} = 3^{36}$. Because the exponents must be equal, solving this problem is easy:
$$2n - 2 = 36$$
$$2n\ \ \ \ = 38$$
$$n\ \ \ \ = 19$$

11. **E** Whenever a problem contains an "average," the first step is to multiply to see what the <u>total</u> is. In this problem, multiply 155 and 4 (total games bowled) to arrived at the total amount of pins scored: 620. Tom needs to average 170 for 6 games, which means he must hit down 170 x 6 = 1020 pins total. He still needs to knock down 400 pins and he has two games to do it in. Divide 400 by 2 and you have the answer. This approach works with all problems containing "average" questions. (The technical term for this type of problem is a "weighted average" problem.)

12. **A** Although this problem appears to resemble Algebra II, it is really much simpler. Whenever you see multiple equations, consider <u>adding</u> them all together. In almost all cases, the answer will appear as if by magic! In this problem, adding the three equations will yield the equation:
$$x = 20$$

13. **D** A simple construction-formula applies here: the sum of any two sides of a triangle must be greater than the third side. In this problem (which is not drawn to scale, so do not assume that you can measure side **p**; it won't be reliable) **p** + 8 must be greater than 10. Because p is an integer, it must be an integer 3 or greater. (By the way, if the question were to ask for the greatest possible value for **p**, it would be found as follows: $8 + 10 > p$; $18 > p$; **p** is therefore less than 18. If **p** were restricted to integers, the greatest possible value for **p** would be 17.) For more practice on this type of problem, try the Skill-Building Prep Quiz on page 80.

14. **A** This type of problem is one of the most difficult to solve unless a strategic approach is taken. Then it becomes very easy, though nonetheless time-consuming. Unless you are a math-wizard and can figure out the problem algebraically, it behooves you to use numbers in place of the variables. For example, try replacing the following:

$r = 20$

$s = 5$

$t = 3$

The key is to understand the problem so you will select appropriate numbers (otherwise, you may find yourself working needlessly with fractions). Given these numbers, we are saying that it takes 20 ounces to fill 5 bottles of perfume. In other words, each bottle contains 4 ounces. With 3 lbs. (that's 48 ounces), you can fill 12 bottles. We now have our answer: 12. All you need to do is replace the values in the choices and see which yields a result of 12:

(A) $16st/r = (16)(5)(3) / 20 = 12$
(B) $rst/16 = (20)(5)(3) / 16 = 300 / 16 = 18.75$
(C) $16r/st = (16)(20) / (5)(3) = 320/15 = 21.33$
(D) $16t - s/r = (16)(3) - 5/20 = 47.75$
(E) $16t/rs = (16)(3) / (20)(5) = 0.48$

The answer can be arrived at with relative ease, but it takes time. For most students, this problem isn't worth the time consumed; however, for those seeking an 800, it is important to realize that even the most difficult SAT Math problem can be readily solved if there is sufficient time.

15. **E** This is a very tricky problem, requiring time and careful work. The only way to be sure you won't miss this is to write out the various letter-combinations. For example, label the flavors C, S, V, and M. Chart out the flavors with these letters and write out the combinations. Be sure you first understand the problem: the order does not matter, but you can have more than one scoop of the same ice cream flavor. Here are the basic combinations: CSV; CSM; SVM; CVM; CCS; CCV; CCM; SSC; SSV; SSM; VVC; VVS; VVM; MMC; MMS; MMV; CCC, SSS, VVV, and MMM. This is simply a very tricky problem that requires careful solving without any help from mathematical formulas! In some instances, the most difficult part of the problem is understanding it; in this case, the most difficult part is solving it correctly!

A Note to Students from Other Lands: An "Alternate Approach"

This is a very appropriate time to introduce an alternate approach to the SAT. Over the past two decades, I have helped many students who have been very weak in Verbal test-taking, either because English was their second language or because they simply lacked basic skills. I found that a modified strategic approach for Verbal and Math needed to be formulated; the following is the alternate approach I have developed for those who have very weak basic Verbal skills:

SENTENCE COMPLETIONS: Do the first half; skip the rest.

ANALOGIES: Do the first half; skip the rest.

READING:
1) Read the italics
2) Answer questions referring to line-numbers (avoid reading the entire passage; focus instead on surrounding line-numbers to answer these questions).
3) Answer any general questions that you feel you can get correct.
4) Skip the rest of the questions.

MATH (all sections):   Do the first half and any that appear easy to answer (for example, those with fewer words and more easy-to-understand illustrations and mathematical symbols); skip the rest.

This novel approach has proven highly successful for those intimidated by the verbal nature of the SAT. The most glaring setback in this approach, however, is that scores will be confined to a range of 350-450 on the Verbal, 400-500 on the Math. For students whose present scores are in the 200-350 range, this is an excellent first step toward raising scores. However, I have also found that students usually do not wish to stick to this approach once they've maximized its potential. Thus, for those who have not been able to break 290, this approach is a sound start; but once you feel comfortable setting your sights beyond 450/Verbal and 500/Math, follow the uncompromising "Karelitz approach" for Verbal and Math and leave the "alternate approach" behind.

Supplementary Skill-Building Prep Quiz
(Mastering the following will help you gain valuable skills to solve a type of problem that appears quite often on the SAT.)

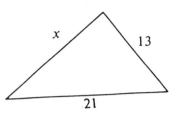

___<𝑥<___

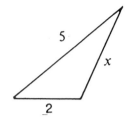

___<𝑥<___

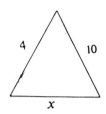

___<𝑥<___

___<𝑥<___

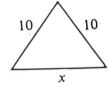

___<𝑥<___

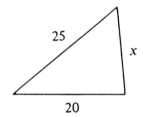

___<𝑥<___

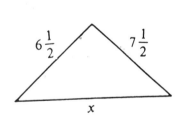

___<𝑥<___

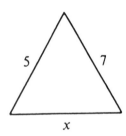

___<𝑥<___

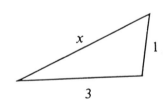

___<𝑥<___

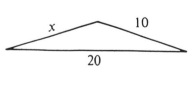

___<𝑥<___

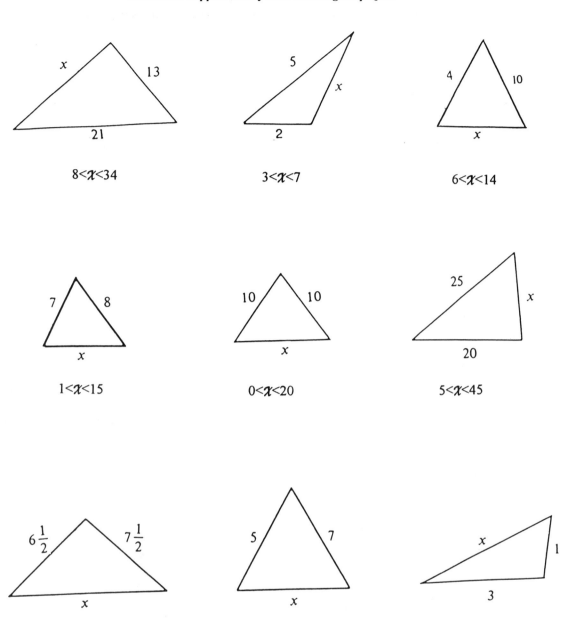

8<*x*<34

3<*x*<7

6<*x*<14

1<*x*<15

0<*x*<20

5<*x*<45

1<*x*<14

2<*x*<12

2<*x*<4

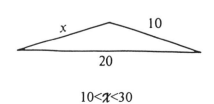

10<*x*<30

Supplementary Skill-Building Prep Quiz
(Minimum/Maximum Problems)
(Mastering the following will help you gain valuable skills to solve a type of problem that appears quite often on the SAT.)

To demonstrate just how easy it is for the SAT test-makers to maintain consistency from test to test, here's a quiz with twelve different questions based on the same given information. These problems could easily appear on different tests without being repetitious, because the answers are not the same. In fact, some of them are downright tricky! Be careful – you might make an avoidable error along the way!

Let **A** = a member of the set {-3, -2, 6} and **B** = a member of the set {-3, 0, 5}

Find: Answer:

   1) the minimum value of **A** + **B**   _____
   2) the maximum value of **A** + **B**   _____
   3) the minimum value of **A** - **B**   _____
   4) the maximum value of **A** - **B**   _____
   5) the minimum value of **B** - **A**   _____
   6) the maximum value of **B** - **A**   _____
   7) the minimum value of **A** x **B**   _____
   8) the maximum value of **A** x **B**   _____
   9) the minimum value of **A/B** (**B** ≠ 0)   _____
 10) the maximum value of **A/B** (**B** ≠ 0) _____
 11) the minimum value of **B/A**   _____
 12) the maximum value of **B/A**   _____

Answers to Supplementary Skill-Building Prep Quiz

If you get 10 or more correct, you've got good SAT problem-solving skills!

1)	-6	7)	-18
2)	11	8)	30
3)	-8	9)	-2
4)	9	10)	1.2
5)	-9	11)	-2.5
6)	8	12)	1.5

MATH MULTIPLE CHOICE:	There are 35 MULTIPLE CHOICE questions on the SAT. They appear in two sections: one containing 25 MULTIPLE CHOICE questions, the other containing 10 MULTIPLE CHOICE questions. They are not mixed together with the other SAT MATH problem types (COLUMN COMPARISONS or GRID-INS).
BEST THING TO DO:	Work carefully. Answer as many as you can solve.
WORST THING TO DO:	Rush and make careless errors. Skip the easy (beginning) problems. Waste time on the difficult (later) problems.
TIME:	Use as much time as you need to solve the easy problems. Don't rush; work carefully. Use any time remaining to: 1) answer problems you feel you can do or 2) go back to check your answers to problems already completed.
STRATEGY-APPROACH:	1) Read the problem, paying special attention to the question. 2) Determine what steps need to be taken to solve the problem. 3) Solve the problem and match your answer with the choices. Use elimination only when appropriate. 4) Recheck the answer with the question, then bubble in your answer on the answer sheet.

SUGGESTIONS FOR LONG-TERM IMPROVEMENT:

Practice and review all errors, taking special note of careless, avoidable mistakes. There is nothing you can study that you don't probably already know. Instead, simply practice and fine-tune your SAT math skills to perfection.

Final Thought

There's only one way to get better and better on the SAT Math: practice and review your errors. And remember that "less is more" (especially if math is your bugaboo); it is better to do fewer and get them correct than to do more and make careless errors along the way. If ever the adage "Practice makes perfect" applies anywhere, it is here on the SAT Math, where you can get better and better simply by avoiding making the same mistakes twice!

SAT Math QUANTITATIVE COMPARISON Problems

The SAT Math portion is unusual not only because it relies heavily on Verbal (reading) skills but also because it contains problems presented in a most unusual format. Much of the difficulty students have in the SAT Math section is understanding what is being asked; solving the problem is usually not difficult once the question is clarified and the directions are understood.

Understanding the rules governing QUANTITATIVE COMPARISON problems will yield immediate score-improvements. In fact, this is usually the portion of the Math test where improvements are greatest and swiftest. Once you know the "ins and outs" of these problems, you will find yourself not wanting to skip any of them. Most are quite simple once you know what the "rules of the game" are.

General Format:

A problem is presented in two-column format. Your task is to determine the value of each column and then compare the two to see which is the greater. The directions are as follows:

A is the answer if the value in Column **A** is greater than that in Column **B**.
B is the answer if the value in Column **B** is greater than that in Column **A**.
C is the answer if the values in both Column A and Column B are the same.
D is the answer if there is insufficient information to tell which Column is greater, or if there is more than one possible answer. (For example, if you find Column A greater than Column B for one variable but not when another is used, then the answer is automatically **D**.)
(There is no **E** answer in this portion.)

To maximize your score on Column Comparisons (a term I prefer over the more general "Quantitative Comparison" moniker) you need to first understand what the problem is asking (similar to the MULTIPLE CHOICE approach) and then simplify any column which may need evaluating. For example, if the problem presents you with the following:

Column A	Column B
6 + 3 x 4	24

you need to evaluate Column **A** (Column **B** is already in its simplest form). Once you have evaluated the columns as needed, the answer is simply a matter of remembering the directions and not making a careless error. In the above problem, the answer is **B** because 6 + 3 x 4 = 18 (remember your order of operations!), and 24 is greater than 18. Therefore, Column **B** is greater; **B** is the correct answer.

In general, of the 15 Column Comparison problems on the SAT the first 10 are usually quite easy to answer correctly; the final 5 may require more careful consideration. Nevertheless, you will probably find every problem in this section worth answering, simply because your only task is to compare which column is greater. Even in more-complicated Column Comparisons, you can often take a logical guess with a high probability of accuracy. This, of course, is not advisable in the Multiple Choice section unless you can eliminate at least one choice. COLUMN COMPARISONS is the only portion of the SAT Math in which logic often plays a greater part than problem-solving.

Strategic Four-Step Problem-Solving "Karelitz Approach":
SAT Math QUANTITATIVE COMPARISON Problems

1) Read the problem (if there is one accompanying the Columns), paying particular attention to what information is being given. For example, if **x** is a positive integer, don't think of using a negative number, a fraction or 0. Simple errors are often the result of careless reading. This first step is very important; don't rush through it!

In addition, don't hesitate to draw your own illustration or chart to better help you set up the problem; the following is a good example of such a problem:

> In a certain 31-day month, Wednesday is the first day of the month.

Column **A**	Column **B**
the number of Wednesdays in that month	the number of Fridays in that month

In this problem, drawing a calendar will help prevent careless errors. With a calendar drawn, you can easily see that there are 5 Wednesdays and 5 Fridays; the answer is **C**.

Though constructed differently, Column Comparison problems and Multiple Choice problems are very similar and should be approached in much the same way: solve them before looking at the choices. (By the way, on the next section – GRID-INS – no choices are given; solving the problems becomes even more imperative. This approach is therefore ideal for all SAT Math problems.)

2) Once you understand what the question wants and have drawn appropriate illustrations and labeled illustrations with relevant information, then you are ready to look at Column **A** and Column **B** to evaluate them. Occasionally, looking ahead at the columns may help you determine how to go about solving the problem. For example,

> **y** is a positive number; $xy = 0$

Column **A**	Column **B**
x/y	0

It might be to your advantage to see what you need to compare before tackling the solving-step. Doing so in this problem could save you both time and effort. Given the information that **xy** = 0 and **y** is a positive number, **x** must be 0. Because 0 divided by any other number is 0, **x/y** and the number 0 (Column **B**) are equal – the answer is **C**. Use your better judgment to determine how to go about solving each problem and you will maximize your results. Avoid wasting time if there is an easier or faster way to solve a problem, but be careful not to rush and thereby make carelessly avoidable mistakes. Work carefully and approach each problem with the problem-solving "Karelitz approach."

In the following problem, answering the question without first carefully solving each column could prove detrimental to your score:

> A bottle containing 15 ounces is one-third full. A
> second bottle containing 23 ounces is one-quarter full.

Column A	Column B
the total amount in ounces of both bottles when full	the total amount in ounces of the second bottle when filled one and a half times

Doing this problem in your head can lead to any number of possible errors. Instead, carefully determine, using the space provided in your test booklet, the total in each bottle when full: 3 x 15 = 45 ounces; 4 x 23 = 92 ounces. The total of the two bottles when each is full is 137 ounces. This number should be written down in Column **A** so you don't forget it. Next, you need to determine what 1½ x 92 is: 3/2 x 92/1 = 138. The answer is now crystal-clear: 138 is greater than 137. Working out every problem on your test booklet helps make the answer easier to determine: there is simply no substitute for showing your work when a problem requires computing or evaluating. For geometry problems with missing angle-measures, take the time to identify the measure of each angle (draw your own illustration if none is provided) before proceeding to compare Column **A** and Column **B**. Work carefully and you will avoid making silly mistakes.

3) Once you have assessed the value of each column, compare them carefully to be sure you have the correct answer. Oftentimes students complete Steps 1 and 2 correctly, then bubble in **B** when they mean to bubble in **A**. This step sounds so obvious but it is often the cause of exasperatingly avoidable errors.

4) Once you have established the answer, stop for one moment to ask yourself if there might be another answer which would in effect render the answer "not enough information"(**D**). Look at the following four problems and see if you can determine which do not have enough information (in other words, are **D**):

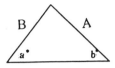

In the triangle above (which is <u>not drawn to scale</u>), angle **a** is greater than angle **b**.

1)

Column **A**	Column **B**
the length of side A	the length of side B

_____

The average (arithmetic mean) of three integers is 15.

2)

Column **A**	Column **B**
the middle integer	15

_____

3)

Column **A**	Column **B**
5X	2X

_____

A hat is on sale for $42, which represents a 30% savings off its original price.

4)

Column **A**	Column **B**
the original cost of the hat	$54.60

_____

These four Column Comparisons show how important it is to think out the problem before trying to arrive at an answer. In problem 1, **A** is the answer; the side opposite a larger angle is always the larger side. In problem 2, the answer is **D**: the problem did not say the integers were consecutive. Careful reading is always a must!

Although this is often the case, it is not always so. For example, <u>none</u> of the following three examples has a **D** answer:

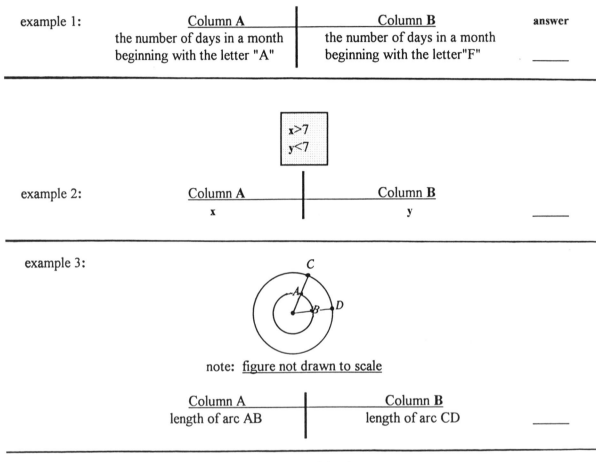

example 1:	Column A	Column B	answer
	the number of days in a month beginning with the letter "A"	the number of days in a month beginning with the letter"F"	_____

x>7
y<7

example 2:	Column A	Column B	
	x	y	_____

example 3:

note: <u>figure not drawn to scale</u>

Column A	Column B	
length of arc AB	length of arc CD	_____

Examples Explained

In the first example, the number of days in <u>A</u>pril is <u>30</u>, the number of days in <u>A</u>ugust is <u>31</u>; however, February contains <u>28</u> or <u>29</u> (leap year) days. In either case, Column A is greater.

In the second example **x** can be any number greater than 7; **y** can be any number less than 7. However, no matter what numbers you use, **x** is <u>always</u> going to be greater than **y**. The answer is **A**.

In the third example, the picture is not drawn to scale; however, we can see that the circle containing arc CD is outside the circle containing arc AB. No matter how the figure is drawn, arc CD will always be outside of (and therefore greater than) arc AB. The answer is **B**.

Returning to our original four problems, the answer to example 3 is **D**: 0 (or a negative number) will result in an answer different from the obvious **A** answer. As demonstrated in our three examples, only when there are two <u>different</u> answers possible is the answer **D**. In problem 4, you need to determine the original cost of the hat. Adding 30% of $42 (which is $12.60) to the sale price = $54.60; the answer appears to be **C**. However, this is an erroneous answer. The correct way to solve it is:

$42 is <u>70%</u> of what number?

$$\frac{42}{x} = \frac{70}{100}$$

The answer to Column A is $60; the answer is **A**.

There are several lessons to be learned by doing these sample problems, but none more glaring than to work <u>carefully</u>. No matter how you prepare to solve the problem, be sure your final answer reflects careful thought, not some half-baked guess. You can save your "educated guesses" for the harder ones if you wish, but your primary concern on the easier/beginning ones is to be sure to get them correct.

(I must admit that most of my errors on SAT Math problems are careless errors. In fact, I commit so many silly errors while explaining Math problems in my classes and workshops that students now refer to them as "Karelitz" errors – it rhymes with "careless"! So remember, work carefully and avoid making those "Karelitz errors"!)

THOSE QUANTITATIVE COMPARISON MATH PROBLEMS ARE TRICKY! HOW COME THERE'S NOT ENOUGH INFORMATION TO TELL IF 2y IS GREATER THAN y? IT LOOKS TWICE AS BIG TO ME.....

BUT WHAT IF y IS O! THEN THEY'RE EQUAL, AND THAT'S WHY THE ANSWER IS "D" — 2y IS NOT ALWAYS LARGER!

ONCE YOU KNOW THESE TRICKS, THE TEST CAN BECOME SO EASY!

HEY, THAT'S WHAT MAKES THE S.A.T. SO CHALLENGING! YOU CAN REALLY IMPROVE YOUR SCORE ONCE YOU KNOW WHAT TO WATCH OUT FOR!

Sample quiz: COLUMN COMPARISONS

<u>Questions 1-15</u> each consists of two quantities, one in Column **A** and one in Column **B**. Comparing the quantities in each Column, enter your answer according to the following directions:

Select
A *if the quantity in Column* **A** *is greater;*
B *if the quantity in Column* **B** *is greater;*
C *if the two quantities are equal;*
D *if the relationship cannot be determined from the information given.*
[there is no **E** *answer in this section]*

Note: In certain questions, given information is centered above the two columns.

	Column **A**	Column **B**	answer
1.	1/3 x 3/5 x 5/9 x 9/11	2/3 x 3/7 x 7/22	_____

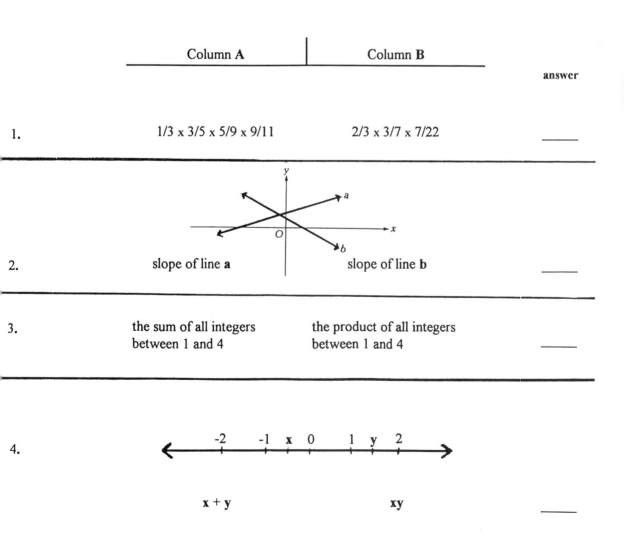

	Column **A**	Column **B**	answer
2.	slope of line **a**	slope of line **b**	_____
3.	the sum of all integers between 1 and 4	the product of all integers between 1 and 4	_____

4.

$$x + y \qquad\qquad xy$$

_____

	Column A	Column B	answer

<table>
<tr><td></td><td colspan="2" style="text-align:center">In 1984, the rainfall in Center City was 49 inches.</td><td></td></tr>
</table>

5.

The number of inches of rainfall during the first nine months of the year

the number of inches of rainfall during the final three months of the year

_____

6. z^2 $z - 2$ _____

$$\begin{array}{r} ABC \\ + BB \\ \hline AAB \end{array}$$

A, B, and C represent different digits

7. $A - 2B$ C _____

An apple tree contains 24 apples. On Tuesday, Fred collected 1/4 of them. On the following day, Sally collected 1/3 of the remaining apples.

8.   the number of apples collected by Fred   the number of apples collected by Sally   _____

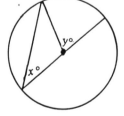

9. $2x$ y _____

10. $\dfrac{3 - r}{2}$ $\dfrac{3 + r}{2}$ _____

Column **A**	Column **B**

answer

note: <u>figure not drawn to scale</u>

11.　　　　　　　a + b　　　　　　　　　　c　　　　　　　_____

12.　　The number of equal angles　　The number of equal angles
　　　　　　in a hexagon　　　　　　　　in a square　　　　_____

13.　　the area of a square　　　the area of a circle
　　　　with side 7　　　　　　　with radius 4　　　　　_____

$$x > 0$$

14.　　　　　$(x^3)^4$　　　　　　　　　$(x^2)^5$　　　　_____

15.

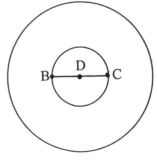

BC is a diameter of Circle **D**. **A** (not pictured) is
a third point on Circle **D**

the ratio of the area of　　　　　　1/3
△ABC to the area of Circle **D**　　　　　　　　　_____

Did you follow the "Karelitz approach" on these problems? More importantly, do you feel you avoided "Karelitz errors"? All in all, I have found that students enjoy this section once they become accustomed to the rules, perhaps because it contains very elementary arithmetic and basic math-applications problems. And though calculators are permitted and often helpful on the SAT, not everyone finds them useful in the Column Comparison section, perhaps because of the nature of the problems themselves: they tend to be simple though tricky. The key to excellence on this portion is to think logically and follow the "Karelitz approach" to problem-solving. The results can indeed be inspiring!

QUANTITATIVE COMPARISON quiz problems explained

1. **C** The key approach to solving all quantitative comparison problems is to actually solve each column and then compare the results. In this very simple problem, each column can be quickly solved through cross-canceling; if you notice a mathematical shortcut, take that route. By the way, if your answer was wrong, stop and review where your error occurred so you don't make the same kind of mistake again.

2. **A** This problem requires a minimum of knowledge about slopes. If the line "climbs," the slope is a positive one; if it "declines," the slope is negative. A "flat" line has a slope of 0; a line that goes "straight up" has "no slope" (also described as "undefined"). The answer to this problem is **A** because a positive value is always greater than a negative one.

3. **B** Mistakes made within the first few problems of this section are likely to be the result of careless errors. Proceed slowly and carefully and you will most likely get all the early (easy) problems correct, which will contribute greatly to your overall math score. Careless errors, on the other hand, will ruin your chances to get off to a good start. In this particular problem, the sum of the integers (2 and 3) is 5; the product of the integers (2 and 3) is 6.

4. **A** A number line is "given information"; that is, you can trust it. You will never see the note "figure not drawn to scale" with a number line or coordinate axis because each is always drawn accurately. Therefore, you can approximate the value of **x** as -1/2 and **y** as +1½. Column **A** is approximately +1, Column **B** is a negative number. You don't need to go any further; **A** is greater.

5. **D** Be careful with problems that do not supply sufficient information. The given facts state that the Center City received 49 inches of rain, but we don't know which months were the rainiest or driest. Do not assume anything not clearly stated or indicated; there is no guarantee that more rain fell in the first nine months than in the final three months of the year.

6. **A** This problem looks easy but can be very tricky. If the problem were to compare Z and 2Z, the answer would be **D** because of exceptions such as 0. In this problem, you need to onsider positive values, negative values, the integer 0 as well as the possibility of fraction-exceptions. Nevertheless, **A** is greater no matter which numbers you substitute for the variable. Many novice test-takers get "lucky" on this one, though most Column Comparison problems favor the experienced over the inexperienced.

7. **C** This is an excellent example of a problem-solving teaser that does not require much math. It is easy to solve, but you need to realize that each variable represents a digit: for example, ABC might represent 234 or 891. Once you know these basic rules, you're ready to solve the problem. With the information presented, it becomes immediately evident C is 0, because the only number that can be added to B to produce B as an answer is 0; B + 0 = B. B + B = A, so we know that A = 2B. Therefore, A - 2B = 0. We have now solved each column; they are of equal value: 0.

8. **C** The most difficult part of this problem is simply figuring out what is being asked. In the last problem, the key was in "problem-solving," but in this word-problem the difficulty lies in reading and comprehending the question. Beyond this, the problem is very easy to solve. Fred has collected 1/4 of 24 apples: 6. Sally has collected 1/3 of what has remained, which is 18 apples. Sally has thus collected 6 apples also. The two amounts are equal.

9. **C** A circle is to be regarded as an accurate drawing, unlike a "square" (which isn't necessarily a square unless all sides are indicated as equal and meet at right angles) or a "right" or "isosceles" triangle (unless it is clearly stated or indicated). The central angle (designated in this problem as **y°**) is always twice the angle measurement of any angle on the circle that has corresponding points on the circle. In this illustration, it is clear that both angles meet at the same points on the circle; therefore, **y** is twice **x**. **2x** is therefore equal in value to **y**.

10. **D** Novices will likely get tricked by this problem; more-experienced test-takers will likely work especially carefully not to get it wrong. Consider these two values and you will see why the answer is **D**: +3 and -3. If you replace **r** with +3, Column **A** will be 0, whereas Column **B** will be 3. But if you substitute -3 for **r**, Column **A** will be 3 and Column **B** will be 0. The answer "changes"; this is proof-positive of a **D** answer.

11. **A** The figure shows a triangle, but there is a warning that the figure is "not drawn to scale." However, remember that the sum of two sides of a triangle must always be greater than the third side, no matter what type of triangle it is. Many forget this basic tenet of triangles and think the answer is **D**; don't be one of these "forgetters"!

12. **D** Although we know that a square contains 4 equal angles, a hexagon can contain 2-6 equal angles, depending on how it is constructed. (Note: A "regular hexagon" is the term for a hexagon with all equal angles/sides.)

13. **B** It may help to illustrate this problem, though the appropriate formulas are really all you need to solve each column. Column **A** is easily found: 49. For column **B**, you need to find the result of $\pi \times 4^2$: approximately $3.14 \times 16 \doteq 50.24$. Again, the two values are not very close; the answer is quite apparent.

14. **D**   The final couple of problems are likely to be the most difficult – or the trickiest, as in this case. $(x^3)^4$ is the same as x^{12}; $(x^2)^5$ is the same as x^{10}. But that's only half the problem; if your answer was **A**, you were fooled. **0** would result in an exception, but because x>0 this value cannot be used. But **1** can! That's all you need to know that Column **A** is not always greater than Column **B**.

15. **B**   This is a rather complicated problem, requiring time and clearheadedness. The best way to approach this problem is to draw point A on the circle, perpendicular to segment BC. This will produce the largest triangle possible. Now you simply need to determine the area of the triangle and the area of the circle, which is not too difficult: Using **r** as the height as well as the radius, you will find the area of the triangle to be $(\frac{1}{2})$ **(r) (2r)** and the area of the circle to be $\pi \times$ **r**^{2}. The ratio of the two areas is thus $\dfrac{\frac{1}{2} \times 2 \times r^2}{\pi\, r^2} = \dfrac{1}{\pi}$.

This simplifies to approximately $\dfrac{1}{3.14}$, which is less that 1/3. The largest possible

triangle therefore cannot match the ratio in Column **B**, and therefore Column **B** is greater in all instances. This problem is not difficult but does require time and effort. For most students, this problem is not worth doing; but for those who seek perfection, this problem (and frankly, any problem on the SAT Math section) is really not all that difficult.

Let's Review

MATH QUANTITATIVE ("Column") COMPARISON:
> There are 15 COLUMN COMPARISON questions on the SAT.

They appear together with the STUDENT-PRODUCED ANSWERS problems as follows:
> #1-15: QUANTITATIVE COMPARISONS
> #16-25: STUDENT-PRODUCED ANSWERS

BEST THING TO DO:
> Work Carefully.
> Try to answer most if not all the questions.

WORST THING TO DO:
> Rush and make careless errors.
> Skip the easy (beginning) problems.
> Spend excessive time on the difficult (later) problems.

TIME:
> Use as much time as you need to solve the easy problems. Don't rush; work carefully, especially on the first (easiest) problems. Don't be afraid to attempt to answer all of the other questions too; you can probably take effective "educated guesses" on even the last (hardest) problems. Unlike the Multiple Choice problems, Column Comparisons rely to a greater extent on logic and common sense; they are all answerable, if time allows. Remember, however, that this section is followed by 10 Student-Produced Answer questions – budget your time accordingly.

STRATEGY-APPROACH:
> 1) Read the problem carefully to comprehend what is being presented and asked.
> 2) Evaluate Column **A** and Column **B**.
> 3) Compare the values of both columns to arrive at an answer.
> 4) Recheck the answer with the question to be sure all variables have been considered. Bubble in your answer on the answer sheet.

SUGGESTIONS FOR LONG-TERM IMPROVEMENT:
> Practice and review your errors, taking special note of "Karelitz errors." This is the best way to approach perfection on this portion of the SAT Math.

Final Thought:

Over the years, many students have told me that the COLUMN COMPARISONS are the easiest problems on the SAT. However, I also know that inexperienced students unfamiliar with this type of problem find COLUMN COMPARISONS to be the most confusing part of the test. This simply goes to show that the SAT is a strategy-test – not an aptitude test – which favors those familiar with its format. In fact, it's a silly test with its own rules, but if you "know how to play the game," you'll score a lot higher than a person who doesn't! The path to SAT success is through practice and review, which over time will allow you to master the art of problem-solving. Only one more portion remains to be confronted and de-mystified: the "riddle of the GRID-INS"!

SAT Math STUDENT-PRODUCED ANSWER Problems

No other portion of the SAT is so misunderstood as the STUDENT-PRODUCED ANSWER problems. Students look upon these 10 problems as tantamount to an invasion from the nether world, as though these questions contain Calculus and beyond. The truth is that these are among the easiest math problems on the SAT. They are elementary word-problems that simply do not offer five choices to select an answer from.

We have already discovered from earlier discussions that SAT Math problems need to be solved before considering the choices. In this section (which I prefer to call GRID-INS because the answers must eventually be written in and bubbled in the answer-grid provided) there are no choices; so when an answer is arrived at, your next step is to simply input it onto the answer sheet. Though elimination is no longer a strategy here, it never was a significant strategy in the other Math portions, anyway. GRID-INS therefore are merely an extension of what has already been encountered on the SAT Math section, though they in fact tend to be even easier in nature than the other SAT Math problems.

As mentioned in previous chapters, the key to mastering the SAT Math is to understand the specific directions. In no other portion is this more true than in the GRID-INS. Therefore, let's review how to answer such questions before we consider a strategic plan of attack.

GRID-INS: How To Answer Them

Here's a problem accompanied by a "grid" in which to write your answer. Though the SAT scoring-computer only looks at the bubbles filled in, it is advisable to write the answer in the boxes as well to prevent a careless error in bubbling. Once you have written the answer in the boxes, there is little chance of bubbling in the wrong answer.

QUESTION: What is one-half of fifteen?

If you wrote your answer as 7½, you are wrong. That would be the same as 71/2 = 35½. The correct answer is either 15/2 or 7.5 (as a decimal). This sounds obvious, but as many as 10% of all first-time test-takers bubble in 71/2. This is the type of error that, once recognized, is easily avoidable; in fact, chances are you will never make this mistake again now that you know how to correctly fill in the grid.

When you approach the GRID-INS section, remember that your primary objective remains the same as with all other SAT Math portions: work carefully and get as many easy problems correct as you can. Use your time wisely and follow the "Karelitz approach" for GRID-INS, which is similar to the approach for other SAT Math problems:

Strategic Four-Step Problem-Solving "Karelitz Approach": SAT MATH GRID-INS Problems

1) Read the problem <u>carefully</u>. Because there are no choices with which to check your work, you need to be sure you know exactly what is being asked. Drawing illustrations or charts is more important than ever before because the answer you come up with will be the one you will be gridding in. There is no "helping hand" (as provided by the five choices in the MULTIPLE CHOICE portion) nor is there the opportunity to make a logical guess (as you can do in the COLUMN COMPARISON portion). You've got to know what you are doing from the very start. Reading the question twice (or even three times) may be the best approach. Don't take this first step lightly; it is the most important step if you want to get the problem correct.

GRID-INS are usually the most "verbal" of all math problems on the SAT; at the same time, they are the easiest in terms of mathematical work. Generally, they appear to look difficult; however, once you begin to comprehend a problem you'll soon notice how simple it really is. The test-makers keep these problems simple because they know that as many as one-fourth of the students taking the SAT have had little or no practice with GRID-INS. (I don't know of a single school that teaches "GRID-INS" in their mathematics curriculum; quite frankly, it is such a strange format that I don't know why anyone would want to do so!) If you can approach each problem knowing that the most difficult part is understanding what is being presented and asked, you will find yourself in the right mind-set to solve the problem easily and correctly.

2) Having read and comprehended the problem being presented, solve it as you best can: sometimes this requires computation; at other times, it requires an illustration; at still other times, common sense may be your best guide. As long as you know what is being asked, you should have little trouble arriving at an answer.

The following is a typical SAT GRID-INS problem. Read the question carefully, then decide how to best go about solving the problem and answering the question. Don't leave any pictures to the imagination; if it helps to illustrate the problem, do so. After all, the test-booklet is meant to be written and drawn on; use it just as though it were scratch paper, which it indeed is.

QUESTION: Line 1 contains three points: A, B and C. C bisects segment AB. If the length of AC is 16, what is the length of segment AB?

If this were a MULTIPLE CHOICE problem, there would be five choices. Even so, looking at the choices before solving this problem would not be advised; the only advantage of having five choices would be to check your answer with the choices to better confirm that your answer is correct. On GRID-INS you are not given five choices, so you must simply input your answer and move on to the next problem.

By the way, multiple choices oftentimes confuse more than they help. In the above problem, the five choices might be:
  (A) 4
  (B) 8
  (C) 12
  (D) 16
  (E) 32

If you set up the problem incorrectly, you are likely to get one of the answers listed (though it is the wrong answer) and if you try to do it without drawing an illustration, you are also likely to chase a wrong answer. Multiple choices do not always help; the key to answering MULTIPLE CHOICE and GRID-IN problems is to <u>solve</u> them. (Incidentally, the answer is <u>not</u> 8, a common response; the correct answer is 32.)

• MYTH #24: Because there is no penalty on GRID-INS, this is like a bonus section.

On the GRID-INS portion, there is no penalty for an incorrect answer; a wrong answer is the same as a skipped answer. However, the fact remains that if you don't get a problem correct, your score falls approximately 10 points; skip all ten problems and you've lost 100 points.

If you understand the question being asked, you should be able to provide a reasonable answer. The only time you should leave a problem unanswered is if you do not understand what it is saying. Time remains your closest ally; don't waste it on problems you are unable to comprehend. Random guessing serves only to waste time as well, because there are no choices to select from. In fact, the odds of guessing a GRID-IN problem correct through random-means are probably the same as picking a winning number in a million-dollar lottery! Therefore, use your time to solve what you can; getting three problems correct is worth much more than guessing ten problems incorrectly.

3) Once you have solved a problem, be sure your answer addresses the question. A common "Karelitz error" occurs when the problem requires solving for x, yet the question asks "What is the value of $2x$?" Once you've solved the problem, take a moment to review the question; this is time well spent.

4) You are now ready to enter your answer onto the grid. Be sure to write your answer on the correct grid; if you are on problem #28, your answer should go on grid #28. This seemingly obvious step is often the cause for costly "Karelitz errors." Work carefully from Step 1 through Step 4 when you are on the GRID-INS portion. Silly, avoidable errors are unfortunately commonplace in this portion of the SAT.

Write the answer carefully in the boxes above the bubbles to avoid careless errors in bubbling, but don't forget that the bubbles <u>must</u> be filled correctly for credit. The bubbles include the digits 0 through 9 as well as a decimal point and fraction bar. You can therefore write fractional answers either as decimals or fractions.

If the answer contains fewer than four digits, you can begin wherever will accommodate the answer. For example, the answer "37" can be filled in the first two columns or the last two, or the middle two. But do not skip a space between numbers. The following are examples of acceptable answers:

THE GRID-IN SECTION IS REALLY EASY, AND THERE'S NO PENALTY FOR A WRONG ANSWER!
YOU'RE RIGHT! IT'S REALLY JUST LIKE THE MULTIPLE CHOICE SECTION EXCEPT THE CHOICES ARE REMOVED.
AND REMEMBER TO ALWAYS READ THE QUESTION CAREFULLY SO YOU KNOW WHAT IS BEING ASKED.
AND IF I DON'T HAVE A CLUE, IS IT WORTH GUESSING ANYWAY? MAYBE I CAN PUT "6.32" AND HOPE TO GET LUCKY.....
DON'T WASTE TIME GUESSING! YOU'D HAVE BETTER ODDS WINNING THE STATE LOTTERY!

If the answer is 9:

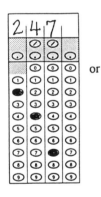 or 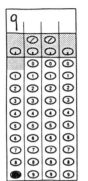 or 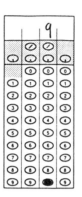 or

If the answer is 247:

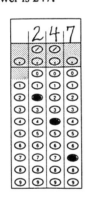

If the answer is 1 3/4:

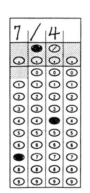 or 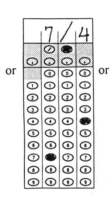 or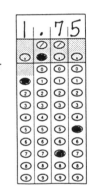

If the answer is 3 1/3:

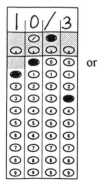

If the answer is 4 5/9:

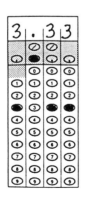 or 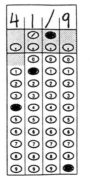 or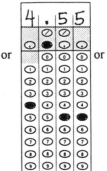

Sample quiz: STUDENT-PRODUCED ANSWERS

The following are typical SAT Math GRID-INS. Proceed carefully and be sure to work out each problem on the test booklet to avoid "Karelitz errors." If you don't understand what a problem is asking, even after a second read-through, skip it and move on. Remember that there is no penalty in this portion; get as many correct as you can.

Directions: *Solve each problem, then write your answer in the grid. No question has a negative answer.*

Note: Some problems may have more than one possible correct answer; in such cases, enter only <u>one</u> answer.

1. What is the difference between the product of the first four positive integers and the sum of the first three positive odd integers?

2. After a team has won 30% of its first twenty games and then wins its next five games, what is its new percent of winning games? (In your answer, disregard the percent sign.)

3. If a 70-foot-long board is cut into three pieces such that the longest piece is twice the length of the middle piece, and the middle piece is three times as long as the shortest piece, how many feet long is the longest piece?

4. If Kalani and Marla each begin running along the same route at the same time but Kalani travels at a pace twice as fast, in how many <u>minutes</u> will Kalani be 8¾ miles ahead if Marla is running at an average pace of 3½ miles per hour?

Questions 5-6 refer to the following chart:

Score	Number of Students
20	3
18	5
14	3
12	3
10	3
9	4

x represents the MEAN score of the students in the chart above, **y** represents the MEDIAN score, and **z** represents the score that is the mode

5. What is the value of **z** - **y**?

6. What is the value of **x** - **y**?

7. If the ratio of the sides of two cubes is 2 : 3 and a side of the larger cube is 6 inches, what is the volume of cubic inches of the smaller cube?

8. Aaron wants to buy some pencils and pens. If the cost each for pencils and pens is 8¢ and 17¢, respectively (tax included), how many total pencils and pens can he buy for exactly $2.06?

9. Sue has a collection of 32 scarves: 4 are green, 6 are blue, and the rest are yellow. If she gives away 5 of them, picked at random, and the first two given away are yellow, the third is green and the fourth is blue, what is the probability that the fifth scarf she picks at random will be blue?

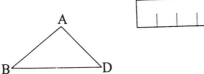

Point C (not pictured) lies on the line segment between B and D

10. If the ratio of the area of △ ABC to the area of △ ABD is 4 : 7 and the length of BC is 9, what is the length of CD?

Were the problems easier than you expected? They tend to be, though for inexperienced test-takers understanding the <u>directions</u> can be the most difficult hurdle to surmount. It's a pity that a test that supposedly measures math-reasoning skills can be presented in such a way that some don't even know what to do. But their disadvantage is your advantage, because now you know exactly what to do and how easy this portion of the SAT really is!

GRID-INS quiz problems explained

1. **15**   Grid-ins are so easy if you just take your time to work out the problem. In this instance, the answer is found by computing as follows:
$$(1 \times 2 \times 3 \times 4) - (1 + 3 + 5) = 24 - 9 = 15.$$

2. **44**   Grid-in problems (officially known as "Student-Produced Answers") require simple problem-solving. In this question, you need to determine that the team has won 6 of its first 20 games (6 is 30% of 20). If it wins its next 5 games, it will have won 11 total out of 25 games played, which is 44%.

3. **42**   In this simple ratio problem (ratios are very popular on the SAT), it is helpful to draw a picture and assign variables to each piece of the board. With x designating the shortest piece, the middle piece is $3x$ and the longest piece is $2 \times 3x = 6x$. You now have the three lengths: x, $3x$ and $6x$, ($10x$ total). $10x = 70$, $x = 7$. The three boards therefore measure 7 feet, 21 feet and 42 feet. Be careful to answer the <u>question</u>; in this problem, they want the length of the <u>longest</u> board.

4. **150**   As with most word problems on the SAT, this one is easy to solve once you understand the question. Always take the time to determine how to go about solving the problem; it will make solving it a lot easier. In this question, Marla is running at an average pace of 3½ miles per hour and Kalani is running at 7 miles per hour. For every hour, Kalani will gain 3½ miles distance. If you divide 8¾ by 3½, you will find how many hours it will take to reach the desired distance:
$35/4 \div 7/2 = 35/4 \times 2/7 = 5/2 = 2½$ hours, which is equivalent to 150 minutes.

5. **4**   As with all multi-part SAT Math questions, it is well worth the time to try to understand what the chart or diagram is indicating. The terms MEAN, MEDIAN and MODE come into play here: the MEAN is the average (found by adding the scores and dividing by the number of students); the MEDIAN is determined by ordering the scores and then finding the one in the middle; the MODE is the score that appears the most often. Once you have these terms under your belt, you are ready to tackle the problem. The MODE (z) is clearly 18, because more students scored 18 than did any other score. To find the MEDIAN, you need to write the scores out or else be aware that the 11th score is the middle one (there are 21 total student scores) : 14 is the MEDIAN. The answer to #5 is now very simple: $18 - 14 = 4$.

6. **0**   This problem is not difficult but will take a minute or two to solve. You know that y is 14, but to find the MEAN you need to add up all the scores and divide by the number of students. In this problem, the work is as follows: $20 \times 3 = 60$; $18 \times 5 = 90$; $14 \times 3 = 42$; $12 \times 3 = 36$; $10 \times 3 = 30$; $9 \times 4 = 36$. The total points is 294, and there are 21 total students; the MEAN therefore is $294 \div 21 = 14$. The value of $x - y = 14 - 14 = 0$.

7. **64** This is a simple teaser which requires clearheadedness. The first thing to realize is that the length of a side of the smaller square is 4 (it is 2/3 the size of a side of larger cube). The volume of a cube is found by cubing the length of the side; therefore, the volume of the smaller cube is 4 x 4 x 4 = 64.

8. **19** This is another simple teaser requiring the proper time and thought to figure out what needs to be done. The question defies any word-problem setup and is moreso a commonsense problem than anything else. The best approach is to take the 17¢ figure and simply begin multiplying it until the remainder, when subtracted from 206, yields a number that is a multiple of 8, the price (in cents) of each pencil. It takes awhile, but it's very solvable;

$$1 \times 17 = 17; \quad 206 - 17 = 189 \text{ (not a multiple of 8)}$$

$$2 \times 17 = 34; \quad 206 - 34 = 172 \text{ (not a multiple of 8)}$$

$$3 \times 17 = 51; \quad 206 - 51 = 155 \text{ (not a multiple of 8)}$$

$$4 \times 17 = 68; \quad 206 - 68 = 138 \text{ (not a multiple of 8)}$$

$$5 \times 17 = 85; \quad 206 - 85 = 121 \text{ (not a multiple of 8)}$$

$$6 \times 17 = 102; \quad 206 - 102 = 104 \text{ (104 } \underline{is} \text{ a multiple of 8)}$$

Therefore, Aaron bought 6 17¢ pens and 13 8¢ pencils (104 ÷ 8 = 13) for a total of 19 items.

9. **5/28** (or **.178** or **.179**) In this ratio problem, some simple computing is necessary to arrive at the answer. To begin with, there are 4 green scarves, 6 blue scarves and 22 yellow scarves. After subtracting the scarves she has given away, Sue is left with 20 yellow scarves, 3 green scarves and 5 blue scarves, for a total of 28 remaining scarves. Now the problem is easy. There are 5 remaining blue scarves out of a total of 28 scarves, so the probability (odds) she will select a blue scarf is 5/28.

10. **6.75** (or **27/4**) In this problem, it is advised that point C be drawn into the illustration for clarity. With the point clearly visible, it is easier to realize that both triangles in question have the same height. Given the formula of the area of a triangle (A = ½bh) and the ratio of the two triangles, you have the equation:

$$\frac{\frac{1}{2} \times BC \times h}{\frac{1}{2} \times BD \times h} = \frac{4}{7}$$

Through simplification,

$$\frac{BC}{BD} = \frac{4}{7}$$

Because BC = 9 (information stated in the problem), through substitution and cross-multiplication, you have:

$$\frac{9}{BD} = \frac{4}{7}$$

$$63 = 4 \times BD$$

$$BD \ \frac{63}{4} = 15 \ ^3/_4$$

The question, however, is asking for the length of **CD**, which is
$$BD - BC, \text{ or } 15\frac{3}{4} - 9 = 6 \ ^3/_4$$

Be careful not to grid this in as 63/4; this would be read as $63 \div 4$, not $6\frac{3}{4}$. The correct grid-inform is either **6.75** or **27/4**.

MATH STUDENT-PRODUCED ANSWERS ("Grid-Ins"):
There are 10 GRID-INS questions on the SAT.

They appear after the 15 COLUMN COMPARISON problems as follows;
#1-15:   COLUMN COMPARISONS
#16-25: GRID-INS

BEST THING TO DO: Work carefully.
Answer as many questions as you can, even if you are not certain of your answer. (There is no penalty for incorrect answers on GRID-INS.)

WORST THING TO DO: Skip the entire GRID-INS portion.
Guess wildly – it is a waste of time.

TIME: Because GRID-INS come at the end of the Math section also containing COLUMN COMPARISONS, you have whatever time remains to answer as many GRID-INS as you can. Work carefully and answer the questions you are able to comprehend. The more you can answer, the better; however, what matters most is how many problems you answer correctly.

STRATEGY-APPROACH: 1) Read (and, preferably, reread) the problem carefully to comprehend what is being presented and asked.
2) Solve the problem, using illustrations as a guide whenever helpful.
3) Check to be sure your answer matches the question being asked.
4) Grid in your answer. (Write it first in the boxes to help avoid "Karelitz errors.")

SUGGESTIONS FOR LONG-TERM IMPROVEMENT:
Practice and review your errors; pay particular attention to "Karelitz errors." By reviewing your mistakes you might find that you need to read the question more carefully, solve the problem more slowly and carefully, or even be more careful when gridding the answer. Practice can shore up these weaknesses, and your score will skyrocket as a result!

Final Thought

+

A Final Word on the Math Section of the SAT

SAT GRID-INS are nothing more than simple word problems which need to be solved without the benefit of five answer-choices. Most can be answered with a minimum of work; oftentimes, all ten are easy to answer correctly if you work carefully. Once you gain the upper hand on this section, you will probably find it to be the easiest portion of the SAT Math.

The SAT Math is a test of common sense and basic mathematical applications. Whatever simple formulas you might need are provided at the start of each Math section, removing the only possible stigma for students weak in Algebra or Geometry. If you like math, you'll find the problems easy; if you dread math, you'll soon realize how high you can score by applying logic and reasoning to answer the questions you know.

A Final Overview Note on the SAT

The SAT is not a "math test"; neither is it a "vocabulary test." It is certainly not an aptitude test, and reading (although a significant ingredient) is not the main focus of the SAT. Instead, this is a test of TIME-MANAGEMENT and common sense. It is a test in which STRATEGIES, not knowledge, will maximize your scores. Having good verbal and math skills certainly helps, but without proper TIME-MANAGEMENT even the most gifted of students will perform poorly. On the other hand, with a proper TIME-MANAGEMENT STRATEGY any student can achieve amazing success on the SAT! Fine-tune your TIME-MANAGEMENT plan of attack and you will MAXIMIZE your SAT scores!

GEE, I REALLY ENJOYED LEARNING ABOUT THE S.A.T. IT'S NOT A HARD TEST, AFTER ALL!
I AGREE. IF YOU BUILD UP YOUR VOCABULARY AND FINE-TUNE YOUR READING AND REASONING SKILLS, YOU'LL DO WELL ON BOTH THE VERBAL AND MATH SECTIONS!
AND THOSE SKILLS WILL ALWAYS BE HELPFUL, EVEN AFTER COLLEGE.
SO TRUE! THAT'S WHY I THINK THE S.A.T. IS SUCH A GOOD TEST; IT ENCOURAGES STUDENTS TO BUILD UP SKILLS THAT WILL BE EVEN MORE VALUABLE AS ONE GETS OLDER!
THANKS FOR ALL THE HELPFUL HINTS!
MY PLEASURE, AND I HOPE TO SEE YOU AT COLLEGE NEXT YEAR! IT'S GOING TO BE A FANTASTIC NEW EXPERIENCE FOR ALL!

The **PSAT** Test of Writing Skills

Although not on the SAT, the PSAT now features a third section, the TEST OF WRITING SKILLS. It is a section worth reviewing because more and more colleges are requiring the SAT-II (Subject Tests), especially the SAT-II ENGLISH test (which includes a student-produced essay as well as a grammar section). The PSAT TEST OF WRITING SKILLS is not in fact a writing test but a GRAMMAR test that quite accurately reflects grammar questions asked on the SAT-II. Because the PSAT is also a scholarship test for those who score extremely high, it becomes necessary to excel in GRAMMAR as well as VERBAL and MATH to now become eligible for PSAT/NMSQT awards.

In addition to the SAT-II ENGLISH test, many colleges also are beginning to require the SAT-II MATH test, which is not a strategy-test (as is the SAT-I MATH TEST, as we've discussed in this book) but a test of basic knowledge of Algebra I and Algebra II, Plane and Solid Geometry, as well as Trigonometry. Fortunately, most of the larger State Universities continue to base their admissions on grades and SAT-I scores and do not require SAT-II scores to be submitted. Nevertheless, taking two or three SAT-II tests can impress colleges, especially if you demonstrate your proficiency by scoring well on the tests. SAT Subject Tests presently offered include: ENGLISH WRITING; ENGLISH LITERATURE; AMERICAN HISTORY & SOCIAL STUDIES; WORLD HISTORY; MATH IC; MATH IIC; BIOLOGY; CHEMISTRY; PHYSICS; FRENCH; SPANISH; MODERN HEBREW; ITALIAN; LATIN; GERMAN; CHINESE; JAPANESE; KOREAN. (Each test is approximately one hour; a maximum of three Subject Tests may be taken during an SAT test-date.) With the recent emphasis by many colleges (and the PSAT) on grammar, it may be well worth the time to investigate this section. (Perhaps it may one day even become part of the SAT-I!)

General Description of the TEST OF WRITING SKILLS

On the TWS (Test of Writing Skills), the first sentences (approximately 20) each contain four underlined words/phrases. Your task is to identify which one of the underlined parts contains a grammatical error. E is the answer if all four underlined portions are grammatically sound. Errors may be found in improper tense-shift, lack of subject/verb agreement, misuse of a word, faulty punctuation, or any other grammatical faux pas the PSAT test-makers can manufacture.

The subsequent dozen or so sentences are structured in a slightly different manner, though the grammatical element remains constant. In these sentences, part or all of the sentence is underlined, followed by four rewrites of the underlined portion. In this portion, you are asked to determine which of the choices is the best in terms of grammar and writing style. A is always the same as the original sentence; the other four are rewrites. One rule proves very helpful in this section: unless there is a grammatical discrepancy, the shortest of the choices is usually the best; the others are probably redundant or unnecessarily verbose. Put simply, if it's short and makes sense, it's probably the best answer.

The final handful of questions relate to a short reading passage, but unlike the Verbal READING portion of the SAT, the questions here are grammar-oriented, not reading-comprehension oriented. Therefore, it is not as important to read the passage as it is to address the grammatical questions associated with it; this is far different from our focus on reading in the Verbal SAT portion.

Despite the three different formats, the TEST OF WRITING SKILLS is consistent throughout in its focus on GRAMMAR. No questions concern spelling (though emphasis is placed on misused words, such as "there" for "their" or "except" for "accept"); in addition, there are no vocabulary questions or analytical reading questions.

TIME: Because this section more closely resembles Verbal than Math, it is important to move quickly rather than slowly-and-carefully on this section. In the first portion, elimination of the correct choices will help determine the grammatically incorrect segment; in the second part, quick elimination of two or three incorrect rewrites will help identify the best answer; and on the last portion (containing the reading passage), a combination of quick reading and elimination will help you arrive at the best answer.

Unlike the Verbal section, however, the TEST OF WRITING SKILLS section does allow adequate time to complete all problems as long as you maintain a brisk pace. In addition, the last part (which contains the reading) is not as vital as is the READING portion of the SAT VERBAL. The questions are not as plentiful and quite frankly are very easy to answer; after all, their primary concern is grammar, not content. In all, the TWS section is fast-paced and quite manageable.

Strategic "Karelitz Approach" to TEST OF WRITING SKILLS

Because there are three different sub-sections in the TWS, you need to be aware of the different directions, as glossed over in the previous page.

PART ONE: choosing the incorrect answer

EXAMPLE: Walking down the street, my books fell. No error
                A   B   C   D   E

The strategy for answering questions of this type is fast and simple:
  1)   Read the sentence quickly to understand what is being said.
  2)   Look for any obvious grammatical error. If you see one, mark the appropriate bubble on your answer sheet and move on to the next question. Take advantage of time-saving easy problems.
  3)   If you don't notice any obvious error, reread the sentence to see if you may have missed something. If you see an error upon the second read-through, mark that answer and move on.
  4)   If you still don't see anything wrong, quickly eliminate the choices that seem correct. If you find them all grammatically and structurally sound, mark E ("no error") and move on.

The answer to the PART ONE sample TWS sentence is **C**.
(<u>My books</u> were not walking down the street!)

PART TWO: choosing the <u>best</u> answer

> EXAMPLE: <u>When he arrived, all his friends came to meet him at the airport.</u>
> (A) When he arrived, all his friends came to meet him at the airport.
> (B) Arriving at the airport, all his friends came to meet him.
> (C) When all his friends came to meet him at the airport, he arrived.
> (D) Arriving at the airport, his friends had come to meet him.
> (E) All his friends came to meet him when he arrived at the airport.

The strategy for answering questions of this type is fast and simple:
1) Read the sentence and ask yourself if it makes sense and is grammatically sound. If you think it is a good sentence, look quickly through and eliminate **B, C, D,** and **E**. Once you have indeed eliminated the other four choices, select **A** on your answer sheet and move on. (**A** is the same as the original sentence and is marked when the original sentence is the best.)
2) If the original sentence does not appear correct, look at the other choices and eliminate those that are obvious in error. After eliminating two or three choices, select the best answer from those that remain and move on.

The answer to the PART TWO sample TWS sentence is **E**.
(The phrase "at the airport" needs to be placed together with "when he arrived"; only **E** addresses this structural requirement.)

PART THREE: selecting the <u>best</u> answer to questions that relate to a given reading passage

In this portion of the TWS, you will need a minute or two to quickly read the passage, gain a general understanding of the nature of the essay and its tone, and perhaps even notice where structural errors exist. Do not spend much time on this first reading because, as with the Verbal READING portion, the key is in answering the questions correctly (through elimination, of course).

The strategy for answering questions in this part of the TWS is quite elementary:
1) Read the passage quickly. Unlike in the Verbal READING portion, skimming may also be feasible at this time to gain a general, superficial understanding of the nature and development of the passage.
2) Answer questions concerned with grammar and those referring to specific line numbers. You may need to read around the lines (as is the case with SAT Verbal READING questions) to gain a fuller context of the question, but you will find the answers to be easy to locate.

3)   If you find an obvious answer, mark it on your answer sheet and move on. If the answer is not obvious, employ the "limited elimination" strategy to better select the "best" answer.

4)   Return to the more general questions. You may need to reread a part of the passage to address a question, but you needn't reread the entire passage (as might be the case when attempting to answer more-difficult SAT Verbal READING questions). Eliminate two or three choices, then select the best answer from what remains. Don't spend much time on any one question; on the other hand, since this is the final part of the TWS you may find that you have ample time to work slowly and carefully (time-management triumphs!).

General TWS Organization

The TWS is organized such that the first problems on each portion are generally the easiest, the final ones the hardest. The reading portion tends to differ and follow the format of the SAT Verbal READING: the first questions tend to embody the earlier part of the essay, the final questions the latter part. But the level of difficulty is not a critical factor on the TWS because of the ample time available to answer all the questions. In addition, all the questions are similar in their grammatical focus, so if you're good in grammar, this section will be a "piece of cake"; if not, you'll no doubt be glad the SAT doesn't feature this section!

The following sample quiz will give you a good idea how proficient you are in the TWS Reading portion. Look over your mistakes so you don't repeat the same errors on the real PSAT. Improving your grammar will invariably aid in developing better writing skills; the two are inextricably bound. If you can get at least two-thirds of the problems correct, you are doing quite well on the TWS.

Sample quiz: TWS Reading

(1) I've always wondered whether realists are pessimists or optimists. (2) To me, a realist is a person who does not place too much reliance on luck; he is aware of the nature of events and has no expectations that a bolt of lightning will come down and strike him with the Midas touch. (3) For him, luck is replaced with effort and resolute consistency. (4) Gamblers never win.

(5) To be an optimist, one must see the best in life and expect the best to occur. (6) But if this optimism is truly compatible with real expectations – not pipe dreams – it can only exist when one's own efforts can generate positive results. (7) An optimist would therefore be as unlikely to expect to win a lottery as would a realist. (8) But while both have a solid grip on reality, the pessimist on the other hand looks upon the future as an impending doom. (9) He does not see any effort capable of generating positive gains. (10) His attitude is the opposite of the dreamer, not the optimist.

(11) The realist is simply an optimist who doesn't openly voice this optimism in the future. (12) Whereas the pessimist feels nothing will turn out for the better, the realist knows that any favorable outcome is dependent upon one's present actions – a view I feel surely is more positive than negative.

DIRECTIONS: *Select the best answer based on content and construction of the previous passage.* (circle your answer)

1. If this essay were written to stimulate discussion in an audience of college philosophy students, which of the following versions of Sentence **1** would most effectively introduce the point in question?
   - (A) I've always wondered whether realists are pessimists or optimists.
   - (B) Realists may be pessimists or they may be optimists.
   - (C) Are realists pessimists or optimists?
   - (D) A discussion worthy of investigation is whether realists are pessimists or optimists.
   - (E) A realist: pessimist or optimist?

2. Which of the following portraits best exemplifies the definition of a realist as presented in Sentence **2**?
   - (A) a gambler at a high stakes table
   - (B) a hardworking automobile mechanic
   - (C) an underachieving student
   - (D) a rich oil magnate
   - (E) a failing businessman

3. In Sentence **8**, who does "both" refer to?
   - (A) the pessimist and realist
   - (B) the realist and dreamer
   - (C) the optimist and dreamer
   - (D) the pessimist and optimist
   - (E) the realist and optimist

4. Which sentence could be omitted from the essay without affecting its tenor?
   - (A) Sentence 1
   - (B) Sentence 4
   - (C) Sentence 7
   - (D) Sentence 10
   - (E) Sentence 11

5. Which two sentences contain contrasting subjects?
   - (A) Sentences 1 and 2
   - (B) Sentences 2 and 3
   - (C) Sentences 5 and 6
   - (D) Sentences 7 and 8
   - (E) Sentences 11 and 12

ANSWERS:

1. **C**   The Reading portion of the TEST OF WRITING SKILLS asks questions relating to grammar, sentence structure, essay development, and content. This first question focuses on content and appropriate tone. Elimination is always the best way to approach such questions; they closely resemble the READING questions on the Verbal section, though they are not as deeply concerned with content. In this question, the key is to determine what type of introductory sentence would be most appropriate for an audience of college philosophy students. It should be direct; it should be focused. **A** places undue emphasis on "I," **D** is too indirect and excessive in length, and **E** is simply not clear in its intent. The decision is between **B** and **C**. One needs to realize that the sentence should stimulate thought but also flow smoothly in transition with the following sentences. **C** is a more stimulating and provocative opening sentence than **B,** and therefore it is the best answer.

2. **B**   This question requires an understanding that a realist relies on "effort and resolute consistency." As is true with line-reference questions in the Verbal READING section, the answer will most likely NOT be in the sentence cited. Don't be fooled by sentence-references or line numbers; they refer to the location of the QUESTION but not necessarily the ANSWER!

3. **E**   Always read the essay quickly before tackling the questions. This will give you an idea what is being discussed and said. Without reading the paragraph, one might think the two referred to are the realist and pessimist, but the previous sentence invalidates any such assumption. The two referred to are the optimist and realist, and both are contrasted in Sentence 8 with the attitudes of the pessimist. To avoid being duped by questions such as this one, you need to allot sufficient time to reread specific parts of the passage.

4. **B**   This type of question often looks to be difficult; in truth, it usually isn't. Of the five choices, one will most likely appear glaringly inappropriate. Don't spend too much time here; select the sentence that is of least importance and move on.

5. **D**   Strictly a grammar issue, this question requires identification of the subjects in each of the five groups of sentences. Here are the subjects:
    Sentences 1 and 2: "I" and "realist"
    Sentences 2 and 3: "realist" and "luck"
    Sentences 5 and 6: "one" and "it"
    Sentences 7 and 8: "optimist" and "pessimist"
    Sentences 11 and 12; "realist" and "realist"
    Now the answer is obvious. Notice that the Verbal READING section does not ask this type of question; this is peculiar to the TEST OF WRITING SKILLS.

TEST OF WRITING SKILLS: There are approximately 40 questions on the PSAT; this section does not appear on the SAT. The first portion requires identification of the grammatically incorrect underlined portion. The next portion requires identification of the grammatically correct sentence-rewrite. The final portion includes a short reading passage together with questions related to its grammatical and organizational correctness.

BEST THING TO DO: Work speedily but carefully.
Answer all questions.

WORST THING TO DO: Skip problems.
Misuse time by progressing too slowly during the first two portions of the TWS, thereby having too little time to address the Reading passage.

TIME: There is ample time to complete the TWS if you move swiftly through the first two portions. The essay-portion does not require too much time to complete, so by setting a moderately fast pace you will have sufficient time to answer all questions.

GENERAL STRATEGY-APPROACH:

(For the Reading-essay section: Read/skim the passage quickly.)
1) Read the sentence/question and look for an obvious answer.
2) If no obvious answer appears, eliminate two or three choices.
3) Select the best answer from those that remain.
4) Bubble in your answer and move on.

SUGGESTIONS FOR LONG-TERM IMPROVEMENT:

Practice and review your errors. Moreso than in any other section, the TWS can be dramatically improved with simple review. Inasmuch as I have seen SAT MATH scores rise 200 points within a month, I have seen TWS results skyrocket in one week! No other section matches the TWS for nearly-identical questions test after test. SAT MATH questions tend to resemble one another from test to test, but TWS questions are so nearly identical that it is a wonder more people don't score perfect on this section. Practice truly makes perfect on the TEST OF WRITING SKILLS!

Directions (1-20): *Select the letter containing a grammatical error. If there is no error, select* **E.** (circle your answer)

1. <u>After</u> an hour of interrogating the suspect, the investigator <u>concludes</u> that the perpetrator
   A   B
   had not <u>yet</u> been <u>apprehended</u>. <u>No error</u>
           C   D   E

2. <u>With</u> his nose totally clogged, he <u>found</u> it <u>most</u> difficult to breathe <u>good</u>. <u>No error</u>
   A   B   C   D   E

3. Alarmed <u>with</u> the lightning, the horses <u>bolted</u> and jumped <u>the fence</u> <u>to freedom</u>. <u>No error</u>
         A   B   C   D   E

4. The stern foreman refused to <u>except</u> any excuses <u>for</u> tardiness <u>or</u> ineptness from his
                              A   B   C
   <u>underlings</u>. <u>No error</u>
     D   E

5. Awarded a medal <u>for</u> bravery, the fireman instead <u>lauded</u> all those <u>that</u> helped <u>in</u> the
               A   B   C   D
   dramatic rescue. <u>No error</u>
               E

6. Never <u>were</u> there more <u>dissenting</u> voices <u>than</u> at the town meeting <u>that</u> afternoon.
        A   B   C   D
   <u>No error</u>
    E

7. He spoke <u>laughingly</u> of his younger days <u>when</u> he and his mates <u>would sneak</u> into a
          A   B   C
   drive-in movie <u>ensconced</u> in the trunk of a friend's car. <u>No error</u>
              D   E

8. Unable <u>to decide</u> <u>between</u> the five delicious flavors <u>of</u> ice cream, he ordered <u>them</u> all.
          A   B   C   D
   <u>No error</u>
    E

9. The candidate <u>refused to budge</u> an inch <u>on</u> his opinions <u>nor</u> even listen to <u>opposing</u>
                A   B   C   D
   viewpoints. <u>No error</u>
             E

10. <u>Either</u> his wife or <u>he</u> would have to stay home <u>to babysit</u> the <u>ailing</u> tot. <u>No error</u>
    A   B   C   D   E

11. After a week out <u>of</u> the hospital, <u>the doctor</u> remarked how <u>good</u> she <u>looked</u>. <u>No error</u>
                      A   B   C   D   E

12. <u>Few</u> in the audience <u>knew</u> <u>who</u> the speaker's insults were <u>directed</u> at. <u>No error</u>
   A   B   C   D   E

13. The witness could not <u>maintain</u> consistency <u>in</u> her account, <u>which</u> strayed <u>away</u> from the
                        A   B   C   D

    truth. <u>No error</u>
          E

14. There <u>is</u> a number of <u>different</u> theories <u>regarding</u> the origin <u>of</u> life. <u>No error</u>
     A   B   C   D   E

15. No one remained <u>after</u> the performance <u>but</u> <u>for</u> the custodian and a few stage <u>hands</u>.
                   A   B   C   D
<u>No error</u>
  E

16. Of the two plants, the <u>one</u> exposed <u>to</u> sunlight <u>grew</u> the <u>best</u>. <u>No error</u>
                      A   B   C   D   E

17. <u>As</u> the bell rang, students quickly <u>jumped</u> to <u>their</u> feet and ran <u>out of</u> the classroom.
  A   B   C   D
<u>No error</u>
  E

18. Prices quickly <u>rose</u> <u>after</u> demand <u>for</u> oil <u>supplies</u> increased. <u>No error</u>
                A B   C   D   E

19. The test <u>covered</u> both early folklore <u>as well as</u> <u>more</u> modern stories of legendary
            A   B   C
    proportion. <u>No error</u>
      D   E

20. The scoutmaster was not certain <u>if</u> one bag <u>or</u> even two bags of rice <u>were</u> enough to feed
                                  A   B   C
    the <u>troop</u>. <u>No error</u>
       D   E

Directions (21-30): *Select the letter of the choice that best expresses the thought of the sentence. If the original sentence is the best, select A.* (circle your answer)

21. Surfing is a sport which is very enjoyable for him on weekends.
    (A) Surfing is a sport which is very enjoyable for him on weekends.
    (B) On weekends, surfing for him is a very enjoyable sport.
    (C) He enjoys surfing on weekends.
    (D) For him on weekends, surfing is a very enjoyable sport.
    (E) On weekends, surfing is enjoyed by him.

22. Election results were questioned as soon as it became clear that not all ballots were counted.
    (A) as soon as it became clear
    (B) as it was becoming clear
    (C) as everyone saw clearly
    (D) when clearly it had become known
    (E) when it became clear

23. The patients were not happy with their food, a few demanding a hearing with the superintendent.
    (A) food, a few demanding
    (B) food and a few were demanding
    (C) food; a few demanding
    (D) food – a few demanding
    (E) food: a few demanding

24. Many dinosaurs were heavier than a truck and ate a lot, too.
    (A) heavier than a truck and ate a lot, too.
    (B) heavier than a truck and had a large appetite.
    (C) heavier and ate more than a truck.
    (D) heavier, with a large appetite, than a truck.
    (E) heavier than a truck and had a larger appetite than one.

25. Unlike his younger cousin who had brown eyes, he had blue ones.
    (A) eyes, he had blue ones.
    (B) eyes, the ones he had were blue.
    (C) eyes and he, blue.
    (D) eyes while his were blue.
    (E) eyes, blue eyes are what he had.

26. <u>Looking both ways, no cars could be seen in either direction.</u>
    (A) Looking both ways, no cars could be seen in either direction.
    (B) No cars could be seen looking in either direction.
    (C) After looking both ways, no cars could be seen in either direction.
    (D) Looking both ways, he could see no cars in either direction.
    (E) In either direction, no cars could be seen by him.

27. On the family vacation, the children enjoyed <u>swimming and being able to spend long evenings playing games.</u>
    (A) swimming and being able to spend long evenings playing games.
    (B) swimming and to be spending long evenings to play games.
    (C) to swim and spend long evenings playing games.
    (D) swimming, spending long evenings, playing games.
    (E) swimming and spending long evenings playing games.

28. The club treasurer refused <u>to be giving out funds unless it was</u> for a good cause.
    (A) to be giving out funds unless it was
    (B) to give out funds unless
    (C) giving out funds unless being
    (D) funds to be given out unless
    (E) unless it was giving funds out

29. If a person cannot accept criticism, <u>you won't ever learn from it.</u>
    (A) you won't ever learn from it.
    (B) nothing will be learned from it.
    (C) he won't ever learn from it.
    (D) it won't teach him anything.
    (E) they won't ever learn from it.

30. The inveterate gambler had several <u>vices, among them being</u> women and alcohol.
    (A) vices; among them being
    (B) vices: among them being
    (C) vices, being
    (D) vices, among them
    (E) vices: including

(1) Waikiki Beach is a landmark in the Hawaiian Islands. (2) Tourists come from far and wide to bask in the sun, chat with fellow visitors, and perhaps even be surfing in one of the most famous spots on the planet.

(3) A tourist is known as a "malihini," whereas kamaainas are the local residents. (4) I wonder if there are such distinctions between native Alaskans, for example, and visitors there. (5) Many tourists wish they could become kamaainas; on the other hand, they often also realize that sitting on the beach day after day is not a rather productive lifestyle. (6) There comes a time when even the laziest of us wants to get back to the daily grind: going to school or work, shopping, and doing other mundane activities.

(7) Maybe paradise has its limitations. (8) The exception, however, is if you can call paradise "home."

Directions (31-35): Select the best answer based on content and construction of the previous passage. (circle your answer)

31. What phrase in Sentence **2** is grammatically inconsistent with the remainder of the sentence?
    (A) far and wide
    (B) bask in the sun
    (C) even be surfing
    (D) one of the most famous
    (E) on the planet

32. Which of the following sentences would best restate the contrast between "malihini" and "kamaaina" mentioned in Sentence **3**?
    (A) Whereas a tourist is known as a "malihini," kamaainas are the local residents.
    (B) Although tourists are "malihinis," local residents are "kamaainas."
    (C) "Malihini" is a tourist and "kamaaina" is a local resident.
    (D) A tourist is known as a "malihini"; "kamaaina" is a local resident.
    (E) A tourist is known as a "malihini"; a local resident is a "kamaaina."

33. To maintain the continuity of the essay, where should Sentence **4** be placed?
    (A) It should remain where it is.
    (B) It should be omitted.
    (C) after Sentence **2**
    (D) after Sentence **5**
    (E) after Sentence **8**

34. What rather silly assumption has been made that lends a humorous overtone to the essay?
    (A) Tourists and local residents are not noticeably different.
    (B) People come to Waikiki Beach to talk with others.
    (C) Lazy people enjoy the daily grind.
    (D) Local residents spend all their days sitting on the beach.
    (E) Paradise can actually be someone's home.

35. Which of the following is/are presented in the essay?
        I. a comparison
        II. a term
        III. a specific reference

    (A) I only
    (B) II only
    (C) I and II
    (D) II and III
    (E) I, II and III

Answers to Sample quiz: TWS

1. B	11. B	21. C	31. C
2. D	12. C	22. E	32. E
3. A	13. D	23. A	33. B
4. A	14. A	24. B	34. D
5. C	15. C	25. A	35. E
6. E	16. D	26. D	
7. E	17. A	27. E	
8. B	18. D	28. B	
9. C	19. B	29. C	
10. E	20. E	30. D	

Final Thought

Grammar is not widely taught during the high school years. Students usually learn the rules of grammar during intermediate school years and forget them as the high school years progress. This is indeed unfortunate because, of all the skills tested on the PSAT, grammar is the one that will have the most lasting effect on one's future, especially if writing (essays, reports, stories, news articles, speeches) will play a significant part in it.

The SAT-II ENGLISH TEST is a requirement for many colleges; practicing and improving your grammar skills can greatly raise this score as well as improve your writing skills. Taking time to polish up on your grammar skills by practicing and reviewing the TWS can really make a difference later on, even after college!

OVERVIEW: Suggestions to Build **SAT** Skills

There are three excellent ways to hone your SAT test-taking skills:

1) Study *The Karelitz SAT Dictionary of One-Word Definitions.*
2) Do CROSSWORD PUZZLES (with a THESAURUS in one hand) to build vocabulary and strengthen concentration skills – good for both VERBAL and MATH.
3) Do LOGIC PROBLEMS for enhanced concentration and problem-solving proficiency. The best LOGIC PUZZLES are published by PENNY PRESS (available in the MAGAZINE section of your favorite supermarket).

These three suggestions are ideal for those who wish to expand upon and improve key SAT skills. However, if your only interest is to raise your SAT scores through effective strategies, then follow the "Karelitz approach" and spare the pain of expanding your brain!

What this Book Is... and Isn't – A Closing Note From the Creator of the "Karelitz Approach" to Taking the SAT

Throughout this book I have steered clear of explanations as to the theoretical makeup of the SAT or of the intricate inner workings of the test. By now, everyone in the land knows what the SAT is used for and why it is and is not a good test. For you, the only reason the SAT is relevant is because it is required by many colleges. Therefore, I have presented concise strategies and techniques that are the product of years of working closely with students in the same predicament. I've gone beyond what other books discuss because I'm sure we have all heard enough about the SAT. This book is a STRATEGY-guide, not another telephone-sized SAT book. If you want to expand your horizons on the SAT by investigating techniques and strategies in greater depth, *The New SAT in 10 Easy Steps* is a good book to pursue. It includes vocabulary quizzes and MATH strategies such as the "0-denominator" and "simplification" techniques as well as "All You Need to Know" battery-tests in Verbal and Math. For most students, however, such detailed strategies are simply unnecessary; you can develop your own strategies equally as well through practice and following this book's simple "Karelitz approach." I have found that overkill can be counterproductive, especially for students who are having enough difficulties following simple strategic approaches; adding more techniques can prove overwhelming.

For those who wish to put your strategies to the test, I recommend the COLLEGE BOARD PUBLICATION *10 Real SATs*. These are actual SATs from the past, complete with answers and scoring charts. No other practice book can compare to the real tests, and College Board reigns supreme in this domain; after all, they are the SAT test-makers! Don't look, however, for strategies in the book. The text explains the test directions and shows how to solve basic problems but does not give strategic information. *The SAT Strategy Guidebook* goes one step further by serving as tutor and coach for those who need more than mere practice and directions. Practice can go only so far before scores level off; guided strategies along with skill-building suggestions can result in score-heights not attainable by simple test-taking.

In my classes and workshops, I present two very distinct strategies for building SAT scores. One involves skill-building and is for highly-motivated students; the other focuses on a strategic test-taking approach (the "Karelitz approach") for students who want to raise SAT scores without putting in too great an effort. Most of my students fall in the latter category – their needs are more pragmatic. For them, the only reason to be taking an SAT-prep class is to raise SAT scores; whatever is learned along the way is secondary and often not valued.

Strangely enough, a change seems to occur in this latter group a year or two later, in the midst of their early skill-building college years. Many students have returned during vacation to thank me for helping them with their reading skills (a la the "finger" technique) and problem-solving skills (primarily through my recommendation of PENNY PRESS puzzles). Even more have found *The Karelitz SAT Dictionary of One-Word Definitions* an invaluable tool for their essay-writing. It's amazing how much can result from what began as simply an SAT-prep class.

In this book, I have unveiled the latest strategic approaches used in my classes and workshops. My hope is that you will be able to benefit from these strategies just as thousands of students have done so through the classes they have taken under my instructorship. It's time to put what you've learned to the test. Register for the next SAT and get ready to see your scores climb. The sooner you begin the SAT journey, the sooner you'll reach your goals. Once you take the SAT, you'll be hooked and will want to take it again and again simply to see how much you can improve.

It's time to take that football and run with it. Opportunity awaits if you're willing to meet the challenge. Go for it!

I know you'll succeed!

CONCISE REVIEW

The following represents the approximate structure of the SAT (variations may occur regarding number of questions in a section) along with a strategy-review.

VERBAL SECTIONS:

30 Questions/30 Minutes

Sentence Completions/Questions #1-9:	Go quickly. Try to answer all questions and get at least half correct. Use "limited elimination" approach. TIME: allot 5 minutes
Analogies/Questions #10-15:	Go quickly. Think "purpose"/"tool"/"same"/etc. Answer all questions. Use "limited elimination" approach TIME: allot 3 minutes
Reading Passages (2)/Questions #16-30:	Follow the 4-Step READING approach (see pages 45-48). TIME: allot all remaining time to this portion

- -

35 Questions/30 Minutes

Sentence Completions/Questions #1-10:	Go quickly. Try to answer all questions and get at least half correct. Use "limited elimination" approach. TIME: allot 5 minutes
Analogies/Questions #11-23:	Go quickly. Think "purpose"/"tool"/"same"/ etc. Answer all questions. Use "limited elimination" approach. TIME: allot 7 minutes
Reading Passage/Questions #24-35:	Follow the 4-Step READING approach. TIME: allot all remaining time to this portion

- -

13 Questions/15 Minutes

Reading Passage (oftentimes the 2-passage comparison reading)/Questions #1-13:	Follow the 4-Step READING approach. TIME: allot all 15 minutes to this portion

on VERBAL : be aggressive

MATH SECTIONS:

25 Questions/30 Minutes

Multiple Choice/Questions #1-25:

Work slowly and carefully.
Do the ones you know (don't skip any of the first half).
In the time remaining, try to do more problems; unless you are good and fast on SAT Math, don't try to do the final five problems – they are not worth the time and effort.
If time remains after doing all you can, recheck each answer to be sure it addresses the <u>question</u>; careless errors may be discovered and corrected.

- -

25 Questions/30 Minutes

Column Comparisons/Questions #1-15:

Work carefully.
Try to answer all questions, but don't spend much time on the final three problems.
<u>TIME: allot 15 minutes</u>

Grid-Ins/Questions #16-25

Work carefully.
Read each problem twice before solving.
Try to answer at least the first five questions.
If time remains, try to do more.
In any remaining time, go back to be sure each answer addresses the <u>question</u>. This is a good opportunity to notice and correct careless errors.
<u>TIME: allot all remaining time to this portion</u>

- -

10 Questions/15 Minutes

Multiple Choice/Questions #1-10:

Work slowly and carefully.
Do the ones you know; try to do at least five problems (especially those in the first half).
In the time remaining, look over and answer any additional problems that you feel you can solve.
Unless you are good on the SAT, do <u>not</u> attempt the final two problems.
If time remains after doing all you can, recheck each answer to be sure it addresses the <u>question</u>.

on MATH: be careful

136

(don't rush!)

STRATEGIC "Karelitz Approach" for Maximum SAT Scoring

VERBAL

<u>Score-Range</u>   <u>Advice</u>

200s-300s: You should not be content with scores in this range.

400s: **(recommended <u>only</u> for students who are very weak or slow in Verbal, or for those for whom English is not the native language)**
Answer the easy (first half) SENTENCE COMPLETIONS and ANALOGIES problems and skip the rest. Use remaining time to complete the READING portion.

500s: **(recommended for those seeking scores acceptable to larger universities and less-competitive colleges)**
Answer all problems – get at least half of them correct. Be sure to follow the TIME-allotments (see page 135) to allow sufficient time for READING.

600s: **(recommended for those seeking scores required by more-competitive colleges and universities as well as for those seeking academic scholarships)**
Besides strategic advice mentioned for 500s, build up your vocabulary and reading skills (for suggestions, see pages 19, 49 and 132). Long-term skill-building is highly recommended because you need to get at least 3/4 of the questions correct to earn a 600.

700s: **(recommended for those seeking scores for scholarships or acceptance into elite colleges)**
To earn a 700, you need at least 90% correct answers. This requires solid skills in vocabulary, reading and time management. Serious long-term skill building is a must!

(allow <u>ample time</u> for READING portion!

MATH

Score-range	Advice

200s-300s: You should not be content with scores in this range.

400s: **(recommended only for students who need only minimal scores to fulfill entrance requirements, or for those extremely weak/slow in math)**
Answer the easy (first half) problems on each section. Work slowly and carefully. Get as many as you can correct, but do not attempt any of the more-difficult problems on the second half of each portion. Show all your work to avoid costly and silly errors.

500s: **(recommended for those seeking scores acceptable to larger universities and less-competitive colleges)**
Answer at least half of the problems (especially the first half), then try to answer a few more. Work slowly and carefully to avoid costly and silly errors, but allow time to attempt some of the second-half problems. Especially critical for success is completing all the COLUMN-COMPARISON problems as well as at least 6 GRID-INS. Do not attempt the final 2 or 3 problems on either of the two MULTIPLE CHOICE sections – the time can be better spent rechecking your work on the earlier problems.

600s: **(recommended for those seeking scores required by more-competitive colleges and universities as well as for those seeking academic scholarships)**
Answer all or almost all the questions. Pay particular attention to accuracy and to answering the question. You need to get at least 3/4 of the problems correct to score a 600.

700+: **(recommended for those seeking scores for scholarships or acceptance into elite and technology colleges)**
To earn a 700, you need at least 90% correct answers. Work carefully and beware of tricky problems, especially toward the end of the COLUMN COMPARISON section. Avoidable mistakes must not occur if you wish to score 700+. Of course, you need to be fast as well as accurate to ensure adequate time to address and solve/answer the final (usually hardest, though often trickiest) questions.

on MATH: be careful

(don't rush!)

CHALLENGING SAT
FINAL EXAM

Answer Sheet

SECTION 1 — VERBAL
30 minutes

1. Ⓐ Ⓑ Ⓒ Ⓓ Ⓔ
2. Ⓐ Ⓑ Ⓒ Ⓓ Ⓔ
3. Ⓐ Ⓑ Ⓒ Ⓓ Ⓔ
4. Ⓐ Ⓑ Ⓒ Ⓓ Ⓔ
5. Ⓐ Ⓑ Ⓒ Ⓓ Ⓔ
6. Ⓐ Ⓑ Ⓒ Ⓓ Ⓔ
7. Ⓐ Ⓑ Ⓒ Ⓓ Ⓔ
8. Ⓐ Ⓑ Ⓒ Ⓓ Ⓔ
9. Ⓐ Ⓑ Ⓒ Ⓓ Ⓔ
10. Ⓐ Ⓑ Ⓒ Ⓓ Ⓔ
11. Ⓐ Ⓑ Ⓒ Ⓓ Ⓔ
12. Ⓐ Ⓑ Ⓒ Ⓓ Ⓔ
13. Ⓐ Ⓑ Ⓒ Ⓓ Ⓔ
14. Ⓐ Ⓑ Ⓒ Ⓓ Ⓔ
15. Ⓐ Ⓑ Ⓒ Ⓓ Ⓔ
16. Ⓐ Ⓑ Ⓒ Ⓓ Ⓔ
17. Ⓐ Ⓑ Ⓒ Ⓓ Ⓔ
18. Ⓐ Ⓑ Ⓒ Ⓓ Ⓔ
19. Ⓐ Ⓑ Ⓒ Ⓓ Ⓔ
20. Ⓐ Ⓑ Ⓒ Ⓓ Ⓔ
21. Ⓐ Ⓑ Ⓒ Ⓓ Ⓔ
22. Ⓐ Ⓑ Ⓒ Ⓓ Ⓔ
23. Ⓐ Ⓑ Ⓒ Ⓓ Ⓔ
24. Ⓐ Ⓑ Ⓒ Ⓓ Ⓔ
25. Ⓐ Ⓑ Ⓒ Ⓓ Ⓔ
26. Ⓐ Ⓑ Ⓒ Ⓓ Ⓔ
27. Ⓐ Ⓑ Ⓒ Ⓓ Ⓔ
28. Ⓐ Ⓑ Ⓒ Ⓓ Ⓔ
29. Ⓐ Ⓑ Ⓒ Ⓓ Ⓔ
30. Ⓐ Ⓑ Ⓒ Ⓓ Ⓔ

SECTION 2 — MATHEMATICS
30 minutes

1. Ⓐ Ⓑ Ⓒ Ⓓ Ⓔ
2. Ⓐ Ⓑ Ⓒ Ⓓ Ⓔ
3. Ⓐ Ⓑ Ⓒ Ⓓ Ⓔ
4. Ⓐ Ⓑ Ⓒ Ⓓ Ⓔ
5. Ⓐ Ⓑ Ⓒ Ⓓ Ⓔ
6. Ⓐ Ⓑ Ⓒ Ⓓ Ⓔ
7. Ⓐ Ⓑ Ⓒ Ⓓ Ⓔ
8. Ⓐ Ⓑ Ⓒ Ⓓ Ⓔ
9. Ⓐ Ⓑ Ⓒ Ⓓ Ⓔ
10. Ⓐ Ⓑ Ⓒ Ⓓ Ⓔ
11. Ⓐ Ⓑ Ⓒ Ⓓ Ⓔ
12. Ⓐ Ⓑ Ⓒ Ⓓ Ⓔ
13. Ⓐ Ⓑ Ⓒ Ⓓ Ⓔ
14. Ⓐ Ⓑ Ⓒ Ⓓ Ⓔ
15. Ⓐ Ⓑ Ⓒ Ⓓ Ⓔ
16. Ⓐ Ⓑ Ⓒ Ⓓ Ⓔ
17. Ⓐ Ⓑ Ⓒ Ⓓ Ⓔ
18. Ⓐ Ⓑ Ⓒ Ⓓ Ⓔ
19. Ⓐ Ⓑ Ⓒ Ⓓ Ⓔ
20. Ⓐ Ⓑ Ⓒ Ⓓ Ⓔ
21. Ⓐ Ⓑ Ⓒ Ⓓ Ⓔ
22. Ⓐ Ⓑ Ⓒ Ⓓ Ⓔ
23. Ⓐ Ⓑ Ⓒ Ⓓ Ⓔ
24. Ⓐ Ⓑ Ⓒ Ⓓ Ⓔ
25. Ⓐ Ⓑ Ⓒ Ⓓ Ⓔ

SECTION 3 — VERBAL
30 minutes

1. Ⓐ Ⓑ Ⓒ Ⓓ Ⓔ
2. Ⓐ Ⓑ Ⓒ Ⓓ Ⓔ
3. Ⓐ Ⓑ Ⓒ Ⓓ Ⓔ
4. Ⓐ Ⓑ Ⓒ Ⓓ Ⓔ
5. Ⓐ Ⓑ Ⓒ Ⓓ Ⓔ
6. Ⓐ Ⓑ Ⓒ Ⓓ Ⓔ
7. Ⓐ Ⓑ Ⓒ Ⓓ Ⓔ
8. Ⓐ Ⓑ Ⓒ Ⓓ Ⓔ
9. Ⓐ Ⓑ Ⓒ Ⓓ Ⓔ
10. Ⓐ Ⓑ Ⓒ Ⓓ Ⓔ
11. Ⓐ Ⓑ Ⓒ Ⓓ Ⓔ
12. Ⓐ Ⓑ Ⓒ Ⓓ Ⓔ
13. Ⓐ Ⓑ Ⓒ Ⓓ Ⓔ
14. Ⓐ Ⓑ Ⓒ Ⓓ Ⓔ
15. Ⓐ Ⓑ Ⓒ Ⓓ Ⓔ
16. Ⓐ Ⓑ Ⓒ Ⓓ Ⓔ
17. Ⓐ Ⓑ Ⓒ Ⓓ Ⓔ
18. Ⓐ Ⓑ Ⓒ Ⓓ Ⓔ
19. Ⓐ Ⓑ Ⓒ Ⓓ Ⓔ
20. Ⓐ Ⓑ Ⓒ Ⓓ Ⓔ
21. Ⓐ Ⓑ Ⓒ Ⓓ Ⓔ
22. Ⓐ Ⓑ Ⓒ Ⓓ Ⓔ
23. Ⓐ Ⓑ Ⓒ Ⓓ Ⓔ
24. Ⓐ Ⓑ Ⓒ Ⓓ Ⓔ
25. Ⓐ Ⓑ Ⓒ Ⓓ Ⓔ
26. Ⓐ Ⓑ Ⓒ Ⓓ Ⓔ
27. Ⓐ Ⓑ Ⓒ Ⓓ Ⓔ
28. Ⓐ Ⓑ Ⓒ Ⓓ Ⓔ
29. Ⓐ Ⓑ Ⓒ Ⓓ Ⓔ
30. Ⓐ Ⓑ Ⓒ Ⓓ Ⓔ
31. Ⓐ Ⓑ Ⓒ Ⓓ Ⓔ
32. Ⓐ Ⓑ Ⓒ Ⓓ Ⓔ
33. Ⓐ Ⓑ Ⓒ Ⓓ Ⓔ
34. Ⓐ Ⓑ Ⓒ Ⓓ Ⓔ
35. Ⓐ Ⓑ Ⓒ Ⓓ Ⓔ

Answer Sheet

SECTION 4 — MATHEMATICS
30 minutes

1. Ⓐ Ⓑ Ⓒ Ⓓ
2. Ⓐ Ⓑ Ⓒ Ⓓ
3. Ⓐ Ⓑ Ⓒ Ⓓ
4. Ⓐ Ⓑ Ⓒ Ⓓ
5. Ⓐ Ⓑ Ⓒ Ⓓ
6. Ⓐ Ⓑ Ⓒ Ⓓ
7. Ⓐ Ⓑ Ⓒ Ⓓ
8. Ⓐ Ⓑ Ⓒ Ⓓ
9. Ⓐ Ⓑ Ⓒ Ⓓ
10. Ⓐ Ⓑ Ⓒ Ⓓ
11. Ⓐ Ⓑ Ⓒ Ⓓ
12. Ⓐ Ⓑ Ⓒ Ⓓ
13. Ⓐ Ⓑ Ⓒ Ⓓ
14. Ⓐ Ⓑ Ⓒ Ⓓ
15. Ⓐ Ⓑ Ⓒ Ⓓ

Only answers entered in the ovals in each grid area will be scored.
You will not receive credit for anything written in the boxes above the ovals.

Answer Sheet

SECTION 5 — VERBAL
15 minutes

1 Ⓐ Ⓑ Ⓒ Ⓓ Ⓔ
2 Ⓐ Ⓑ Ⓒ Ⓓ Ⓔ
3 Ⓐ Ⓑ Ⓒ Ⓓ Ⓔ
4 Ⓐ Ⓑ Ⓒ Ⓓ Ⓔ
5 Ⓐ Ⓑ Ⓒ Ⓓ Ⓔ
6 Ⓐ Ⓑ Ⓒ Ⓓ Ⓔ
7 Ⓐ Ⓑ Ⓒ Ⓓ Ⓔ
8 Ⓐ Ⓑ Ⓒ Ⓓ Ⓔ
9 Ⓐ Ⓑ Ⓒ Ⓓ Ⓔ
10 Ⓐ Ⓑ Ⓒ Ⓓ Ⓔ
11 Ⓐ Ⓑ Ⓒ Ⓓ Ⓔ
12 Ⓐ Ⓑ Ⓒ Ⓓ Ⓔ
13 Ⓐ Ⓑ Ⓒ Ⓓ Ⓔ

SECTION 6 — MATHEMATICS
15 minutes

1 Ⓐ Ⓑ Ⓒ Ⓓ Ⓔ
2 Ⓐ Ⓑ Ⓒ Ⓓ Ⓔ
3 Ⓐ Ⓑ Ⓒ Ⓓ Ⓔ
4 Ⓐ Ⓑ Ⓒ Ⓓ Ⓔ
5 Ⓐ Ⓑ Ⓒ Ⓓ Ⓔ
6 Ⓐ Ⓑ Ⓒ Ⓓ Ⓔ
7 Ⓐ Ⓑ Ⓒ Ⓓ Ⓔ
8 Ⓐ Ⓑ Ⓒ Ⓓ Ⓔ
9 Ⓐ Ⓑ Ⓒ Ⓓ Ⓔ
10 Ⓐ Ⓑ Ⓒ Ⓓ Ⓔ

SECTION 1
VERBAL
30 minutes - 30 questions

SENTENCE COMPLETIONS (select the letter whose word(s) <u>best</u> complete the thought of the sentence)

1. When lightning strikes, it is ___ to seek shelter and not ___ oneself to the risk of electrocution.
   (A) advisable...expose
   (B) unacceptable...present
   (C) proposed...delay
   (D) uncommon...condemn
   (E) cautioned...remove

2. Fishermen are highly ___ upon the seas for their ___.
   (A) focused...solutions
   (B) uncertain...survival
   (C) dependent...livelihood
   (D) critical...safety
   (E) excited...future

3. Diamonds are ___ for both their ___ and appeal.
   (A) valued...tranquillity
   (B) denounced...rarity
   (C) criticized...abundance
   (D) secretive...mystery
   (E) renowned...durability

6. Ample time has been _____ for a discussion of ways to conserve our rain forests; it is now time to ___ our ideas for a cleaner tomorrow.
   (A) expended...spurn
   (B) reserved...dispense
   (C) obscured...scrutinize
   (D) allocated...actuate
   (E) delineated...refute

5. Tired of the ___ living conditions in her rundown apartment, Terry notified her landlord that she was packing her belongings and moving into lodging elsewhere.
   (A) servile
   (B) squalid
   (C) inane
   (D) enviable
   (E) moot

6. Known for her extravagance and ___ during her years of movie stardom, Marlene Dietrich surprised the public with her later ___ lifestyle.
   (A) decadence..apathetic
   (B) control...dramatic
   (C) daring...indifferent
   (D) objectivity...unimpressive
   (E) pomp...reclusive

7. Given but one option, MacAbee realized the necessity of ___ a scheme he would earlier have deemed ___.
   (A) relinquishing...whimsical
   (B) perpetrating...unconscionable
   (C) condescending...derelict
   (D) masterminding...exemplary
   (E) terminating...unmarketable

8. Supporters ___ the arrival of the new, more demanding principal as the long-awaited ____ to an age-old problem of moral decay in the school.
   (A) heralded...panacea
   (B) consecrated...retribution
   (C) reconciled...foreboding
   (D) commemorated...awakening
   (E) condoned...resolution

9. Jeremy's ___ and ___ behavior made him the delight of none of his prim and proper aunts.
   - (A) obdurate...eloquent
   - (B) sedulous...belligerent
   - (C) collaborative...indelicate
   - (D) crass...churlish
   - (E) indignant...intrepid

ANALOGIES *(select the letter whose words best express a relationship similar to that expressed by the words in capital letters)*

10. CAKE: ICING::
    - (A) puzzle: solution
    - (B) present: ribbon
    - (C) window: glass
    - (D) steak: meat
    - (E) lake: shoreline

11. DOCTOR: HEAL::
    - (A) plumber: cook
    - (B) politician: regulate
    - (C) astronaut: fly
    - (D) burglar: insure
    - (E) instructor: teach

12. FOLD: CREASE::
    - (A) rip: tear
    - (B) reproduce: distribute
    - (C) reveal: defend
    - (D) clean: recycle
    - (E) expand: distort

13. FULFILLMENT: FUTILE::
    - (A) reward: encouraging
    - (B) significance: mysterious
    - (C) deprivation: acceptable
    - (D) excellence: substandard
    - (E) restraint: disobedient

14. PARIAH: EXILE::
    - (A) aggressor: attack
    - (B) idol: deify
    - (C) sage: discredit
    - (D) victim: abase
    - (E) somnambulist: imprison

15. DECREPIT: AGE::
    - (A) riddled: answers
    - (B) radiated: enlightenment
    - (C) clichéd: overuse
    - (D) atrophied: growth
    - (E) blemished: size

Lemmings possess one of the most inexplicable drives, described in the following passage.

line

No rodent has baffled man more than that belonging to the family Cricetidae, tribe Lemmini. Known throughout Europe and North America as lemmings, these small, mice-like creatures have taken upon themselves, for reason unbeknownst to any but perhaps themselves, a migratory trail whose final steps are self-destruction.
5   Far from a fairy-tale journey, their mission does not end "happily ever after," for their chosen destination -- their Mecca* -- is the ocean, a refuge for fish but not for land-loving rodents.

The farmlands of Norway and Sweden are the most common sites for inundations of lemmings, heading instinctively towards the Atlantic Ocean or the Gulf of Bothnia. Down
10   from the highlands they advance -- "falling out of the sky," Norwegian lore accounts -- steadily but slowly increasing in numbers as they approach the shorelines. Stray packs join the onrush, and the ensuing stampede assumes an almost-maniacal nature crossing streams and lakes several miles wide, trampling anything in their way. As if driven to their destination by an obsessive compulsion, these individually harmless balls of fluff become
15   a formidable adversary for all that stand in their way and a machine of devastation for the grassy fields and farmlands which provide the ravenous herd with life-sustaining nutrients.

The unorthodox lemming migration is not a safe travel for many of the rodents themselves. Farm animals attack the lemmings, whose presence threatens their very food supply. Wild animals and birds of prey relish the lemmings' arrival as a welcome meal.
20   Meanwhile, man represents one of the greatest threats, seeking to exterminate them for much the same reason as do the farm animals. The lemmings' diurnal feeding comes at a time when competition for food is most fierce and farmers are most vigilant. All in all, the lemming migration, lasting in total from one to two years, resembles that of the early American pioneer settlers: long, dangerous and "no turning back."
25   Lemmings are a restless, courageously uncompromising lot whose pugnacious spirit propels them onwards, undaunted by geographical and predatorial obstacles. Paradoxically, all their efforts lead them not to a paradise -- or, as some authorities have proposed, to a land which once offered abundant food supplies before being covered by oceans of water -- but to their demise. What may once have been an exodus from
30   overcrowded, underfed conditions to vast grasslands has now become much the opposite: a journey to destruction.

*The religious capital of Saudi Arabia and spiritual center of Islam;
in general, any desired destination of a pilgrimage.

READING (select the letter of the choice that best answers the question, based on what is stated or implied in the previous passage)

16. According to the passage, which of the following is true?

    I.   Lemmings eat during the day.
    II. The lemming migration lasts up to a couple of years.
    III. Humans safeguard lemming migrations towards the ocean.

    (A) I only
    (B) II only
    (C) III only
    (D) I and II only
    (E) II and III only

17. Which of the following scenes would most likely reflect the nature of the lemming during their ocean-bound migration?
    (A) scurrying to safety to avoid an unexpected gust of wind
    (B) fighting among themselves for leadership on the migration
    (C) casually feasting on the farmland vegetation
    (D) hurrying without regard to safety to cover as much territory possible
    (E) carefully watching over their offspring

18. In the context of the passage, "inundations" (line 8) most closely means
    (A) feeding cycles
    (B) destruction
    (C) falling from great heights
    (D) migrations
    (E) swarms

19. Why might some Norwegians believe that lemmings come "out of the sky"?
    (A) The rodents' ability to jump makes it appear they are descending from the clouds.
    (B) The vast swarm descends from the hills towards the seas almost as if a lemming "flood" has occurred.
    (C) Lemmings have a limited ability to fly during migrations.
    (D) Many lemmings are found crushed to death, explained only by having suffered a sudden descent.
    (E) During the migration, there are no birds to be found.

20. According to the passage, what is the primary difference in the reasons man and wild animals pursue the lemming?
    (A) Lemmings compete with man for food; they provide food for wild animals.
    (B) Lemmings threaten man's food supply; they interfere with the feeding habits of wild animals.
    (C) Lemmings bring diseases to man; they feed off the young of wild animals.
    (D) Man pursues lemmings in sport; wild animals pursue them for survival.
    (E) Lemmings threaten man's existence; they threaten the food supply of wild animals.

21. It can be inferred from the passage that the lemmings' journey shares no fairy-tale ending because
    (A) many lemmings die along the way.
    (B) their trek is rooted in fact, not fiction.
    (C) they meet a tragic fate.
    (D) they must compete with fish for continued survival.
    (E) the food supplies are not as abundant as in eons earlier.

22. The best title for this passage would be
    (A) The Lemmings' Fight For Food
    (B) Lemmings: Survival Through Migration
    (C) Land Of The Lemmings
    (D) The Indomitably Courageous Lemming
    (E) The Mystery Of The Lemming Migration

The following passage is an excerpt from a story about a teenager's road to self-discovery.

line

I presented the ring to Janet in a most unusual way, asking her to hand me the ketchup and then intercepting her delivery.

"You have the softest skin of anyone I have ever met," I added as her eyes met mine. "But I know what would make it even more attractive."

5   Janet was confused for a moment, but only a moment as I moved the golden band from my finger onto hers. She flinched initially, uncertain of my intention, but then surrendered herself to my amorous display. "Do you want to go somewhere tonight?" I continued cautiously.

With the aplomb of a cheerleader, Janet replied "Why not? The evening is young and the drive-in is open. You have anything particular in mind?"

10   A thousand juvenile thoughts raced through my mind as I contemplated the mischief we had masterminded in the seventh grade, Janet and I building a reputation as the havoc-wreakers of Johnson Intermediate. The incident at Jerry's Deli earned us both the respect from our peers and fear from the establishment, an enemy we had conspired to overthrow together. Few remembered for long just what it was we had cleverly concocted, but the aura of our triumph

15   over a world of puritanism and traditional values continued to encircle us for the remainder of the schoolyear. We were saviors, we were the chosen duo -- Batman and Batgirl -- whose mission it was to rid Gotham City of adult tyranny and instead herald a new youthful leadership in the land. True, our approach wasn't very mature; in fact, it was downright sophomoric. But in one single act of mutual bravado, Janet and I let Philadelphia know we would not be

20   silenced.

We had accomplished so much in the seventh grade, but one inescapable obstacle came crashing down on me in the course of two years' passing. No, it was not the law, nor was it any single person. The culprit was time, and I was its most unsuspecting victim. Janet was not just "another guy" anymore; she had blossomed to full radiance. She was a gem whom I had once

25   known as a marble; she was an angel with whom I had once committed deviltry.

So much had come between us -- her sports, my academic involvement -- but I never wanted the bond between us to end. Ever. But things had changed. My interests lay elsewhere, though deep inside I yearned for the companion I once knew. The words that came forth were from my alter ego, my adult self endeavoring to readjust to life as a young man.

30   "Maybe we can sneak into the second show," I began searchingly, "and then ask someone if we can sit in the back of their van." I took a deep, silent breath, wondering if she comprehended my innuendo. And yet, I myself wondered what it was I truly wanted.

"Van?" Janet replied politely, as if setting me up for a punch line. "Do you really think we can accomplish anything stuck in the back of somebody's van?"

35   I was taken aback. Janet wasn't interested in my adult attempts to express feelings I wasn't yet ready for. She knew me for who I was, and probably who I always will be. There was magic in the air for the first time since Jerry's; we were still on the same wavelength.

23. What can be assumed regarding the speaker and Janet?
    (A) They have met only recently.
    (B) They have been going steady for at least one year.
    (C) Janet was not expecting to receive a ring from the speaker.
    (D) Janet is more shy and amorous than the speaker.
    (E) They are both enrolled in the same classes.

24. The setting of this passage would most likely be
    (A) in a hallway between classes
    (B) in Johnson Intermediate
    (C) at a drive-in movie
    (D) in Gotham City
    (E) in a high school cafeteria

25. What information is given concerning the incident Janet and the narrator hatched in the seventh grade?
    (A) no details are presented
    (B) Jerry was also involved
    (C) no one was injured
    (D) they were never caught
    (E) they wore masks

26. How do the speaker and Janet envision the van (line 31)?
    (A) Both view it as the perfect place from which to watch the drive-in movie.
    (B) Both see it as an opportunity to get to know one another better.
    (C) The speaker envisions it in an amorous light, but Janet has other ideas.
    (D) The speaker sees it as a source for mischief, but Janet sees it as trouble brewing.
    (E) Both are ambivalent toward the van.

27. Which of the following best sums up the series of events as seen by the speaker?
    (A) shocking with an ironic undertone
    (B) sadly anticipated
    (C) juvenile and frustrating
    (D) unexpectedly satisfying
    (E) romantic but discouraging

28. In the context of the passage, "aplomb" (line 8) most closely means
    (A) poise
    (B) cautiousness
    (C) attractiveness
    (D) explosiveness
    (E) eloquence

29. What is the narrator's intent in calling Janet "a marble" (line 25)?
    (A) to maintain that she was never a real person
    (B) to show how she was before she changed with time
    (C) to admit frankly that he never fully understood who she really was
    (D) to reveal that she was once less than perfect
    (E) to recall how she was a childhood companion

30. Which question is answered for the speaker in the passage?
    (A) Am I really in love?
    (B) Is there a way to express how I feel?
    (C) Has time changed our friendship?
    (D) Will we ever understand ourselves?
    (E) Will a drive-in movie really satisfy my desire?

The following information is for your reference - *it is provided on every SAT*

A circle measures 360°
A straight line measures 180°
The sum of the angles of a triangle is always 180°

Definition of symbols:
= *equal to*
≠ *not equal to*
< *less than*
> *greater than*
≤ *less than or equal to*
≥ *more than or equal to*
∥ *parallel to*
⊥ *perpendicular to*

all numbers used are real numbers

FORMULAS

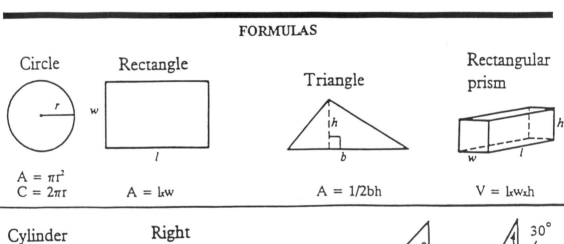

Circle

$A = \pi r^2$
$C = 2\pi r$

Rectangle

$A = lw$

Triangle

$A = 1/2bh$

Rectangular prism

$V = lwh$

Cylinder

$V = \pi r^2 h$

Right triangle

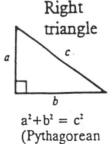

$a^2 + b^2 = c^2$
(Pythagorean Formula)

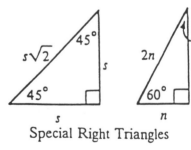

Special Right Triangles

SECTION 2
MATHEMATICS
30 minutes - 25 questions
MULTIPLE CHOICE PROBLEMS

1. $\dfrac{1032}{2} + \dfrac{363}{2} =$

   (A) $\dfrac{1032 + 363}{2}$

   (B) $2(1032 + 363)$

   (C) $1032 + 363$

   (D) $\dfrac{1032 + 363}{4}$

   (E) $\dfrac{1032}{2} + \dfrac{2}{363}$

3. $(10+10+10)(10+10)(10)(10-10)(10-10-10) =$

   (A) -100
   (B) -1
   (C) 0
   (D) 1
   (E) 100

2.

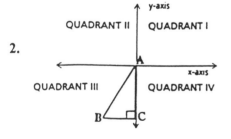

What are possible coordinates for C?
   (A) (-4, 0)
   (B) (0, 4)
   (C) (3, -3)
   (D) (-3, -5)
   (E) (0, - 4)

4. Vince went surfing for 2 1/2 hours at Pipeline. If he concluded surfing at 1:17 p.m., at what time did he begin surfing?
   (A) 11:27 a.m.
   (B) 10:47 a.m.
   (C) 10:27 a.m.
   (D) 9:47 a.m.
   (E) 9:27 a.m.

5. In the number 14.96, if the unit's digit and tenth's digit are switched, what is the change in the value of the number?
    (A) -5.5
    (B) +4.5
    (C) +5.5
    (D) +27.0
    (E) +79.2

6. If a $5 bill is used to pay for 6 pens individually priced at 60¢ and 7 pencils individually priced at 13¢ (tax included in all prices), what is the minimum number of coins - consisting of quarters, dimes, nickels and pennies - given as change?
    (A) 4
    (B) 5
    (C) 6
    (D) 7
    (E) 8

7. -.3 is between all of the following EXCEPT
    (A) -1/3 and -1/2
    (B) -1/3 and -1/4
    (C) -1/6 and -1/3
    (D) -1/4 and -1/2
    (E) -1/4 and -2/3

In problems #8-9, let represent four distinct positive integers as indicated by **m**, **n**, **p** and **r** such that the value of the operation is defined as follows:

$$m^2 + 2r = n^2 - p$$

8. What is the value of **r** in the following illustration?
    (A) 2
    (B) 4
    (C) 6
    (D) 7
    (E) 8

9. Which of the following values for m and n satisfy the illustration?
    (A) m=9; n=8
    (B) m=8; n=9
    (C) m=24; n=0
    (D) m=4; n=8
    (E) m=5; n=7

10. The average (arithmetic mean) of 1/3, 1/6 and 1/9 is
    (A) 1/18
    (B) 1/6
    (C) 33/18
    (D) 11/18
    (E) 11/54

11. What is the difference between the largest and smallest four-digit number that can be made using each of the digits 6, 8, 9 and 8?
    (A) 2997
    (B) 2898
    (C) 2988
    (D) 2097
    (E) 3007

$$F = 9/5 \ C + 32$$
$$C = 5/9 \ (F-32)$$

Consult this chart for questions 12-14

12. Given the above temperature-conversion formula for Fahrenheit and Celsius, what would 50°C be in F°?
    (A) 10
    (B) 60
    (C) 100
    (D) 122
    (E) 172

13. What temperature in C° corresponds with a reading of 0° F?
    (A) -32
    (B) -17 7/9
    (C) 0
    (D) 24 5/9
    (E) 32

14. Which of the following represents the coldest temperature?
    (A) -2°C
    (B) -31°F + 24°C
    (C) 31°F
    (D) 80°C - 140°F
    (E) 59°F - 15°C

15. What is the maximum possible area of a quadrilateral whose perimeter measures 20 inches?
    (A) 25 square inches
    (B) $8\sqrt{5}$ square inches
    (C) 20 square inches
    (D) 16 square inches
    (E) It cannot be determined from the information given.

16. If $x^2+y^2=17$, and $xy=-4$, then $(x+y)^2 =$
    (A) 0
    (B) 4
    (C) 9
    (D) 13
    (E) 25

17. Rodney, a fireman at a nearby station, works for three consecutive days and then has the following two days off. [For example, if Rodney works Thursday, Friday and Saturday, he has days off on Sunday and Monday, returning to work on Tuesday.] If Rodney returns to work on Saturday, November 2nd, which of the following two consecutive days will be days off?
    (A) Tues./Wed. 11/26-11/27
    (B) Mon./Tues. 11/11-11/12
    (C) Wed./Thurs. 11/20-11/21
    (D) Thurs./Fri. 11/28-11/29
    (E) Sat./Sun. 11/16-11/17

18. The results of a vote were in the ratio 6:5:2 for candidates **A**, **B**, and **C** respectively. What was the margin of difference between candidates **A** and **C** in a community of 910 voters?

    (A) 70 votes
    (B) 110 votes
    (C) 210 votes
    (D) 280 votes
    (E) 630 votes

19.

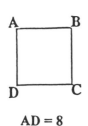

AD = 8

If the midpoints (not shown) of each of the sides of square ABCD are connected, what will be the area of the newly constructed inner square?
(A) 16
(B) $16\sqrt{2}$
(C) $64 - 16\sqrt{2}$
(D) 32
(E) 48

20.

$$3x+2y-z = 6$$
$$3y+2z-4x = 15$$
$$2x-4y-z = 9$$

In terms of y, x =
(A) $2y/3 + 20$
(B) $30 - y$ ✓
(C) $30 - 2y/3$
(D) $2y - 12$
(E) $y/2 + 30$

21.

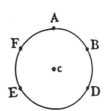

In the figure above, a circle is divided into arcs such that the length of :
$\overset{\frown}{AB} = 1/2\overset{\frown}{AD} = 1/3\overset{\frown}{BE} = \overset{\frown}{EF} = \overset{\frown}{FA}$.
If the circumference of the circle is 18 units, what is the unit measure of $\overset{\frown}{FB}$?

(A) 15
(B) 12
(C) 9
(D) 6
(E) 3

22. If the remainder of a number divided by 3 is 2, which of the following can be the remainder of four times the number, divided by 9?
  ✓ I. 2
     II. 5
     III. 8

(A) neither I, II or III
✓ (B) I only
(C) I and II
(D) II and III
(E) I, II and III

23. Coming off a freeway and into a residential district, Mrs. Davidson always slows down at a consistent rate, reducing her speed by 10% every block. If her speed exiting a freeway is 50 miles per hour, in how many blocks will her speed have first slowed to less than 35 m.p.h.?
(A) 2
✓(B) 3
(C) 4
(D) 5
(E) 6

24. If it takes 4 globs and 3 flobs to build one clob, how many complete clobs can Henry build for $20 if the cost of the ingredients is as follows:
       3 globs for $1
       4 flobs for $1
[note: globs and flobs can only be purchased in multiples listed; tax is included in the above prices]
(A) 7
(B) 8
(C) 9
(D) 10
(E) 11

25. Concentric circles are drawn so that each larger circle has a radius 50% greater than the previous, smaller circle. If the innermost circle has a radius of x, what is the area of the 3rd circle from the center?
✓(A) $\dfrac{81\pi\, x^2}{16}$

(B) $\dfrac{9\pi\, x^2}{16}$

(C) $\dfrac{9\pi\, x^2}{4}$

(D) $16\pi x^2$

(E) $\dfrac{81\pi\, x^2}{4}$

SECTION 3
VERBAL
30 minutes - 35 questions

SENTENCE COMPLETIONS (*select the letter whose word(s) best complete the thought of the sentence*)

1. The origin of the universe continues to ___ even the most ___ scientists.
   (A) alarm...dramatic
   (B) offend...peaceful
   (C) challenge...disagreeable
   (D) convince...supportive
   (E) baffle...knowledgeable

2. Louis XIV maintained a ___ reign over his people, demanding ___ and severely punishing those who disobeyed.
   (A) disciplined...anarchy
   (B) benevolent...simplicity
   (C) consistent...discord
   (D) tyrannical...subservience
   (E) harsh...animosity

3. There is no better place to seek ___ from a world of ___ than to escape to the confines of a library.
   (A) retaliation...pacifism
   (B) sanctuary...ignorance
   (C) compromise...impropriety
   (D) deference...intolerance
   (E) salutation...histrionics

4. To ___ for his ___ physical stature, actor Alan Ladd would often wear platform shoes for added height.
   (A) overcome...elevated
   (B) enhance...brawny
   (C) lament...obese
   (D) compensate...diminutive
   (E) accommodate...petite

5. Paradoxically, Christmas is the time of year when most people ___ about for three weeks so they can enjoy the ___ of one day.
   (A) ponder...repose
   (B) dawdle...vigilance
   (C) scurry...solace
   (D) fret...privilege
   (E) shuffle...bustle

6. ___ by six successive losses to the Chargers, the Falcons rose to the occasion to defeat their ___ rivals in front of the largest home-crowd of the season.
   (A) Undaunted...perennial
   (B) Stimulated...antagonistic
   (C) Disillusioned...invulnerable
   (D) Reproached...elusive
   (E) Confronted...timid

7. Hawaii is a land ___ in ancient cultural history and unique tradition folklore.
   (A) obscured
   (B) rejuvenated
   (C) negligent
   (D) steeped
   (E) impoverished

8. An effective tabloid writer must avoid the ___ in favor of more ___ and controversial subject matter.
   (A) erratic...inevitable
   (B) bland...impartial
   (C) complacent...obligatory
   (D) rabble...disenchanting
   (E) mundane...sensational

9. Losing air speed midway through the flight will ___ what is already a ___ dilemma.
   (A) deteriorate...convoluted
   (B) vilify...predisposed
   (C) exacerbate...precarious
   (D) appease...digressive
   (E) mitigate...harrowing

10. Unable to experience the thrills of professional sports firsthand, "couch potato" viewers instead envision themselves as one of their heros to seek ____ gratification.
    (A) conciliatory
    (B) nefarious
    (C) vicarious
    (D) concupiscent
    (E) eleemosynary

ANALOGIES *(select the letter whose words **best** express a relationship similar to that expressed by the words in capital letters)*

11. AIR: BREATHE::
    (A) feet: walk
    (B) sound: hear
    (C) food: purchase
    (D) detergent: clean
    (E) water: splash

12. VOLUME: LOUDEST::
    (A) depth: highest
    (B) amount: largest
    (C) perfection: extreme
    (D) center: utmost
    (E) silence: happiest

13. AMBITION: SUCCEED::
    (A) concern: pacify
    (B) fortitude: endure
    (C) optimism: follow
    (D) enthusiasm: excite
    (E) caution: rebel

14. DIE: CUBE::
    (A) earth: circle
    (B) box: pyramid
    (C) sugar: square
    (D) can: cylinder
    (E) gem: diamond

15. LIPSTICK: LIPS::
    (A) food: stomach
    (B) soap: hands
    (C) haircut: hair
    (D) pupil: eyes
    (E) rouge: cheeks

16. CENTIPEDE: PINCERS::
    (A) spider: web
    (B) shark: gills
    (C) lobster: claws
    (D) ostrich: legs
    (E) termite: teeth

17. SPOKE: WHEEL::
    (A) stem: leaf
    (B) page: book
    (C) dial: gauge
    (D) rung: ladder
    (E) sprocket: chain

18. INFLAMMABLE: RESISTANT::
    (A) lengthy: burdensome
    (B) uniform: unbalanced
    (C) superficial: magnificent
    (D) unlikely: questioned
    (E) invaluable: priceless

19. SOLDER: DETACH::
    (A) reinforce: weaken
    (B) emblazon: enhance
    (C) align: control
    (D) raze: demolish
    (E) safeguard: disassociate

20. POLICEMAN: ENDANGER::
    (A) manager: disorganize
    (B) actor: forget
    (C) accountant: calculate
    (D) fireman: protect
    (E) lawyer: disbar

21. PROLIX: WORDY::
    (A) malefic: kind
    (B) diffident: conceited
    (C) ingenious: idiotic
    (D) disinterested: biased
    (E) lethargic: sluggish

22. CREVASSE: ICE::
    (A) splinter: wood
    (B) shank: handle
    (C) shard: heat
    (D) slag: metal
    (E) fissure: rock

23. PARSIMONIOUS: MUNIFICENT::
    (A) introverted: gregarious
    (B) mendacious: grandiose
    (C) loquacious: disputatious
    (D) lugubrious: sullen
    (E) skeptical: beneficent

In the following passage, the power of nuclear energy is discussed.

line

Energy has become man's most valuable commodity -- and limited resource -- in the 20th century. With the depletion of oil reserves, alternate sources have been investigated. One possible solution has come from the result of chemical combinations, creating explosive energy capable of supplying electricity and electrical power for an indefinite period of time. Such a power

5   burst may be witnessed by the explosion produced when TNT creates an electron disturbance in the atom's molecular structure. Investigation into such atom-related explosions, an area of science called nuclear physics, has revealed greater potential energy than from simple electrical, gravitational and magnetic forces; and today it has led us into an even newer age of nuclear fission and fusion, offering unlimited sources of power for future expansion and continued survival.

10   The power of nuclear fission was first demonstrated under controlled conditions on December 2, 1942, then unleashed in all its fury on July 16, 1945, in a test explosion of an atomic bomb in New Mexico. One month later Hiroshima, Japan, became the target of a similar bomb, leveling the city and destroying all forms of life in its wake. These explosions proved themselves far greater and far more powerful than those earlier produced with TNT due to the nature of the

15   explosions. Unlike the less-destructive breaking of the outer electron structure of the atom, nuclear fission involves a spontaneous splitting of the heavier nucleus into two or more lighter pieces. This process generates greater levels of heat, resulting in a more spectacular end-result. Thus, as the atomic bomb showed the world the scope of its blast, so too did it present itself as a source of power that, when harnessed judiciously, could light cities and charge generators

20   without end.

Even more recently, a more powerful form of nuclear energy has been explored: nuclear fusion. Unlike its counterpart which breaks up the nucleus, fusion involves the union of two nuclei to create a heavier one. The results are breathtaking. For example, through the fusion of deuterium (heavy hydrogen) in one cubic foot of water, approximately 280,000,000 B.T.U. of

25   energy can be produced -- the same amount that would require the burning of ten tons of coal. A ton of granite can, through fusion, produce nine times the energy of a ton of coal in the furnace. Given the vast quantities of water and of granite available, including its energy-rich uranium and thorium elements, man can through the process of fusion produce sufficient energy to ensure millions of years of worry-free survival, an inexhaustible supply for future technological demands.

30   Atomic power does not come, however, without its dangers. To produce the energy which may one day serve the needs of the world, the construction of a breeder reactor has proven necessary to contain one of its unwelcome by-products: radioactivity. This deadly release presented itself most visibly during the first atomic bomb explosion in the form of a 40,000-foot-high mushroom cloud. The inordinately great loss of life shortly thereafter in Hiroshima and

35   Nagasaki more clearly displayed the potential danger of radiation from such heat-generated bombs; nearly 400,000 persons were killed or injured in the two attacks and by the ensuing radioactive fallout.

Given the power of today's nuclear bombs buried deep in secret silos worldwide, it is time to more clearly manage what we have created. Although the potential advantages of nuclear

40   energy dwarf those of conventional means, the negative potential also hangs above us like a cloud, reminding us that that which provides can also destroy. The power contained in the nuclear processes of energy-production can ensure survival for man, but without proper safeguards and controls, it can destroy the civilization of man in a flash.

READING (*select the letter of the choice that best answers the question, based on what is stated or implied in the previous passage*)

24. The passage is primarily concerned with
    (A) the high loss of life related to misuse of atomic energy.
    (B) the procedure employed to harness energy through fission and fusion techniques.
    (C) the potential of nuclear energy.
    (D) events leading up to modern fusion.
    (E) atomic energy and radioactivity.

25. It can be inferred from the passage that fusion is not used more widely because
    (A) sources are not readily available.
    (B) the process is still being investigated and developed.
    (C) energy cannot be stored for long-term use.
    (D) the need has not yet arisen for such auxiliary techniques.
    (E) salt in the ocean precludes effective use of fusion.

26. Which of the following can be inferred from the passage?
    I.   If man can limit the destructive potential of producing heat-energy, the world will no longer suffer energy shortages.
    II. Fusion may one day be responsible for the destruction of the human race.
    III. Uranium is the primary ingredient necessary in the process involving fusion.

    (A) I only
    (B) II only
    (C) I and II only
    (D) I and III only
    (E) I, II and III

27. Which of the following best describes the development of the article?
    (A) The first three paragraphs explain the topic; the final two cite graphic illustrations.
    (B) The first paragraph builds up the argument; the remaining paragraphs cite pros and cons to the argument.
    (C) The first three paragraphs defend nuclear fusion; the final two subtly oppose it.
    (D) The first three paragraphs expand the topic; the final two soberly document the gravity of the issue.
    (E) The first paragraph introduces key points, each of which is enumerated in subsequent paragraphs through specific incidents.

28. What is the specific difference between the processes involving fission and fusion?
    (A) Fission involves the electron; fusion involves the nucleus.
    (B) Fission divides the core; fusion combines cores.
    (C) Fission splits the neutron; fusion counteracts the neutron.
    (D) Fission requires heat; fusion requires water.
    (E) Fission produces an electrical charge; fusion produces a heat-generated charge.

29. The passage implies that the purpose for a nuclear breeder reactor is to
    (A) avoid contamination of the air.
    (B) maximize the productivity of the process.
    (C) serve the needs of the world.
    (D) monitor safe and unsafe conditions.
    (E) manage and stabilize the proper amounts of energy being released.

30. The underlying message presented by the author can best be restated by the aphorism
    (A) people in glass houses shouldn't throw stones.
    (B) when the cat's away, the mice will play.
    (C) too many cooks spoil the soup.
    (D) a penny saved is a penny earned.
    (E) he who laughs last, laughs loudest.

31. With what other phrase is "in a flash" (line 43) most closely associated?
    (A) "inordinately great loss of life" (line 34)
    (B) "an electron disturbance" (line 5)
    (C) "could light cities" (line 19)
    (D) "a 40,000-foot-high mushroom cloud" (lines 33-34)
    (E) "atomic bomb explosion" (line 33)

32. Which of the following would be the best title for the passage?
    (A) Living With Nuclear Energy
    (B) The Dangers of Atomic Energy
    (C) Fission vs. Fusion
    (D) Atomic Power: Its Potential for Global Salvation or Destruction
    (E) The Atom: Man's Greatest Energy Source

33. Which of the following is used in the passage?
    I.   Specific, dated references
    II. Direct claim by an expert
    III. Simile

    (A) I only
    (B) I and II
    (C) I and III
    (D) II and III
    (E) III only

34. Comparing the energy-production through fusion and non-nuclear techniques, it can be inferred from the passage that 1/4 ton of granite would, through fusion,
    (A) generate roughly as much energy as would the burning of a ton of coal.
    (B) require an equal amount of coal to generate nine times the total output.
    (C) result in 70,000,000 more B.T.U. of energy than would the burning of 1/4 ton of coal.
    (D) cause a 10,000 foot mushroom cloud.
    (E) produce energy equivalent to the burning of 2.25 tons of coal.

35. The author of the passage is most likely
    (A) an informed, objective reporter.
    (B) a scientist directly involved in atomic experimentation.
    (C) an opponent of thermonuclear energy.
    (D) a spokesperson for the atomic energy producers.
    (E) an entrepreneur encouraging unrestricted exploration into new sources of energy.

The following information is for your reference - *it is provided on every SAT*

A circle measures 360°
A straight line measures 180°
The sum of the angles of a triangle is always 180°

Definition of symbols:
= *equal to*
≠ *not equal to*
< *less than*
> *greater than*
≤ *less than or equal to*
≥ *more than or equal to*
‖ *parallel to*
⊥ *perpendicular to*

all numbers used are real numbers

FORMULAS

Circle

$A = \pi r^2$
$C = 2\pi r$

Rectangle

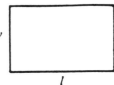

$A = lw$

Triangle

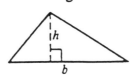

$A = 1/2bh$

Rectangular prism

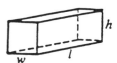

$V = lwh$

Cylinder

$V = \pi r^2 h$

Right triangle

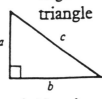

$a^2 + b^2 = c^2$
(Pythagorean Formula)

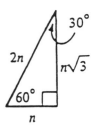

Special Right Triangles

SECTION 4
MATHEMATICS
30 minutes - 25 questions

<u>Questions 1-15</u> each consists of two quantities, one in Column A and one in Column B. Comparing the quantities in each Column, bubble the appropriate oval on the answer sheet according to the following directions:

Select
A if the quantity in Column A is greater;
B if the quantity in Column B is greater;
C if the two quantities are equal;
D if the relationship cannot be determined from the information given.
[there is no E answer in this section]

| Note: In certain questions, given information is centered above the two columns. |

QUANTITATIVE COMPARISON PROBLEMS

<u>Column A</u>	<u>Column B</u>		<u>Column A</u>	<u>Column B</u>

1. $\sqrt{30}$ $\sqrt{5} + \sqrt{25}$

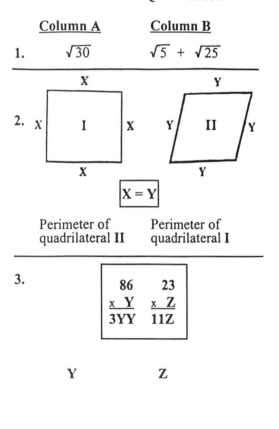

$$X = Y$$

Perimeter of   Perimeter of
quadrilateral **II**   quadrilateral **I**

3.

86	23
x **Y**	x **Z**
3YY	11Z

Y   Z

4.

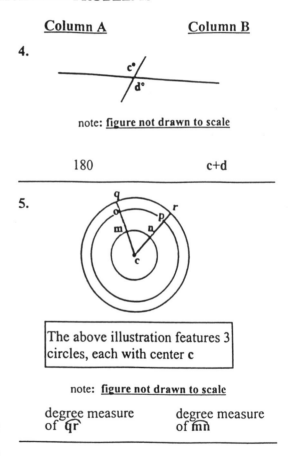

note: **figure not drawn to scale**

180   c+d

5.

The above illustration features 3 circles, each with center **c**

note: **figure not drawn to scale**

degree measure   degree measure
of q̂r   of m̂n

164

Column A	Column B

6.

$$\frac{1}{x}$$ $$\frac{x}{1}$$

7.

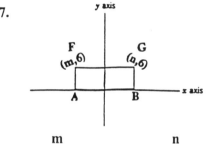

m   n

8.

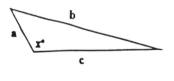

note: **figure not drawn to scale**

a/c   a/b

Column A	Column B

9.

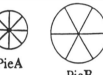

9x - 3y   15

10.

PieA   PieB

Pie A is 1/2 the total area of Pie B.
Pie A is divided into 8 slices of equal area;
Pie B is divided into 6 slices of equal area.

the total area   the total area
of 7 slices of   of 3 slices of
Pie **A**   Pie **B**

11.

Touchdown = 6 points
Extra-point kick = 1 point

Terry scored six touchdowns, and Jay successfully kicked 50% of the extra-point attempts.

total number of   39
points scored
in the game

Column A	Column B

12.

Heavenly Valley had forty-nine inches of snow in December.

In inches, the average monthly snowfall in Heavenly Valley for the entire year.

4

Column A	Column B

14.

$A = \{3, 5, 7, 9, 11\}$ $B = \{2, 4, 6, 8, 10\}$

The number of prime integers in set **A**

The number of composite (non-prime) integers in set **B**

15.

☆X is defined for all integers X as $$\frac{X^2}{2-X}$$

0

The average (arithmetic mean) of $-☆3$ and $☆3$

13.

CD = 2
DB = 5

note: **figure not drawn to scale**

area of semicircle **C**

area of △ABD

STUDENT-PRODUCED ANSWERS

Directions: Solve each problem, then mark the appropriate ovals in the special grid corresponding with your answer. Mark only one oval per column. No question has a negative answer.

Note: Some problems may have more than one possible correct answer; in such cases, grid only <u>one</u> answer.

16. $7 + 3 - 6 \div 4 =$

19. If $1/c - 1/4 = 1/12$, then $c =$

17. Written in decimal form, $21\frac{1}{2}\% =$

20. If each side of a square is increased by 4 inches, the area of the newly formed square is 49 sq. inches. How many inches is the perimeter of the original square?

18.

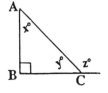

If $AB = BC$, then $z =$

21. In thirteen football games, Johnston High scored the following points: **14, 28, 31, 26, 0, 14, 6, 48, 21, 14, 3, 28, 27.** If **A** represents the median of the points scored, and **B** represents the mode of the points scored, what is the value of **A - B**?

22. What is the slope of a line containing the points (8,2) and (1,-2)?

23. A boy noted the various colors of passing cars, observing the following: Of the first twenty cars, a quarter were red, a fifth were white, one tenth were black, and the rest were of other colors.

Of this total amount, what was the ratio of red cars and black cars to those that were neither red nor black?

24. If a 3-pound batch of cookies requires 28 ounces of butter and 4 ounces of sugar, what percent of the total weight of the batch do the other ingredients comprise? [16 ounces = 1 pound]

25.

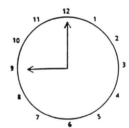

The time on the above clock is 9:00. What is the number of degrees of the largest angle formed by the hands of the clock when the time is <u>4:00</u>?

SECTION 5
VERBAL
15 minutes - 13 questions

The role language plays in our lives is investigated in the following two passages. In the first essay, the origin, purpose and value of language are explored. The second essay takes a more pragmatic look at language and communication in our society.

Passage 1
line

There is no single, uncontested theory regarding how language is acquired and whether it determines an individual's consciousness or is a product of the degree of perception inherent in a being at birth. Cognitive theorists and supporters of the nativist approach may forever maintain divergent views, yet they do share a common bond in the fundamental significance of language:
5 It is the primary means through which man is able to communicate with one another, share the past and ponder the future. A more haunting question, however, concerns the purpose of language -- whether it is used in a volitional manner or is a means for manipulation of and by others.

In his operant conditioning theory, B.F. Skinner contended that verbal behavior is conditioned by the consequences it effects. When consequences are positive, the behavior is reinforced; when
10 results are negative, the behavior is weakened, oftentimes to the point of extinction. Following this premise, an individual's use of language therefore depends greatly upon the audience to whom it is addressed. We might assume that a criminal would find little value espousing standard, conventional registers and would instead gain a safer footing in a more colloquial argot, one establishing for himself an aura of brute strength and unbridled hostility against any oppressor. In
15 contrast, one could hardly expect a college professor to address his listeners as if they were threats to his security. The language uttered therefore bears close resemblance to the environmental conditions about which the individual is exposed, serving to achieve whatever desired purpose the situation dictates.

Let us now turn our focus to the young child who, in the critical first years of life, acquires
20 those precious first words that shall forever form the foundation for further verbal development. In this setting, the role of the parents' language is of crucial significance, followed closely by that of siblings. Because the child is not aware that he or she is acquiring a language, his receptiveness to words is as open as if a recorder soaking in the sounds around it; there is no censoring device, no benefit of experience to screen out what might prove detrimental in the long run from what
25 might yield beneficial results.

Child behavior psychologist Jean Piaget noted that what the child learns about language is determined by what he already knows of the world. Yet, this empirical wisdom does not avail him of the proper words to use to describe his worldly interpretations. The role of instructor becomes invariably the pivotal ingredient toward showing baby the most socially rewarding way to present
30 such observations for others to share. We find Skinner's operant conditioning not only at the helm, but necessarily so for the betterment of the individual. Abraham Maslow listed hierarchical human needs, ranging from the basic physical needs (air, food, water) to higher needs of personal

169

fulfillment (purpose in life, and ultimately what Maslow terms "self-actualization"), and no better example of a means toward achieving these ends can be found than in the very words one uses
35   to gain such needs. "Water" is a word that satisfies one desire; "Mama" will produce a more abstract and equally desired comfort. Whether the words are initially introduced by the conditioner or the child himself, the ultimate use of these words is to affect one's environment to gain whatever the individual seeks.

     Theorists may forever strive to prove through objective analysis that language exists in the
40   imagination before it is tapped, or expands the imagination as it is introduced. But such debates are moot in the larger scheme of life, for the first few formative years provide only the introduction to life's complete story. The turning point comes not early in life, as cognitivists and nativists may contend, but instead at an age in which the individual is fully aware of the potential available to him. The subject of conditioning becomes the manipulator well after the road of life has begun,
45   though well before the road has been traveled.

Passage 2
line

     Have the linguists and behaviorists had enough after years of arguing how people learn to communicate? Language is purported to be a system that helps bridge differences, strengthen bonds, and create harmony and agreement amongst the multitudes. And yet, centuries of honing our language skills have done little to bring peace to the world, with even less hope for improved
50   relations in the future. There is, in fact, something inherently wrong with language: It is evaluated and criticized on a biased scale. Those who do not conform to standard White English are deemed socially inferior, whereas those who do modify their perceptions to accommodate the white-collar lifestyle are lauded.

     Hundreds of studies have been conducted to expose differences in language acquisition,
55   including second-language learning. The results have been quantified and correlated to prove the validity of the findings, but what have we discovered: that "The sun hot is" is inferior to "The sun is hot"? Doesn't each represent what each speaker wishes to say, even though one may not be as grammatically accurate? Is the latter speaker "smarter" than the former one; is one more "acceptable" in the social world than the other? If we are to commend the speaker who most
60   appropriately addresses our own cultural dictates, then we should travel to Alaska and comment on how pretty the snow looks. An Eskimo is sure to wonder how we can be so naïve to have but one word for an entity as diverse as "snow." In a land where snow comes in many shades and densities, we "standard Americans" must therefore be deemed as cretins unable to discern amongst the variety of the most prolifically falling substance from the sky.

65   There is no evidence to indicate that the language one uses reflects a greater awareness of the world around him, or within him. Humanity shares the same birth and death experience; few have ever thought to claim that only those with "standard English" will be let through heaven's gates, though I'm sure there are one or two after life-linguists around who wish they were the gatekeepers. We must then assume that this life experience is a universally shared period, with
70   basic emotions inherent in all peoples. Why then is such a flurry of attention brought upon the

manner in which people speak; why do pedantic pigeon-holers continue to stress that the differences between people's perceptions of life are directly related to the words they have been taught. If we were to smash a hammer on the foot of the most learned and reputable of linguists, would he not utter the same yowl as the laborer and the bus driver?

75   Language serves a vital function for all individuals and all communities: It offers the means through which to express how we feel and communicate what we believe, in order to better seek harmony with the world around us. Let's not argue over or even attempt to resolve differences where they do not exist. The best argument for dissolving further discussion is to observe the elaborate bickering of the linguists themselves, a sad commentary on the state of affairs in the

80   world today. Were we instead to focus our attention on bringing social groups closer together, the world would be a better place in which to live.

READING *(select the letter of the choice that best answers the question, based on what is stated or implied in the previous passages)*

1. What is the primary purpose of paragraph 1 in Passage 1?
   (A) It points out the uselessness of pursuing the argument further.
   (B) It dispels two previously supported beliefs concerning the issue.
   (C) It debunks the divergent nature of two schools of thought.
   (D) It introduces the issue by presenting contrasting theories.
   (E) It establishes the author's attitude on the subject.

2. The author of Passage 1 implies that a criminal uses colloquial language because he considers others
   (A) targets for manipulation
   (B) highly imaginative
   (C) threats to his security
   (D) intimate allies
   (E) of inferior intelligence

3. According to Passage 1, who might be considered the second most important influence in a young child's verbal development?
   (A) his parents
   (B) an aunt
   (C) a neighborhood friend
   (D) a brother or sister
   (E) a teacher

4. What does the author of Passage 1 conclude regarding the role of language as a means to manipulate an individual?
   (A) The language a person hears and mimics at an early age controls his later development.
   (B) A person learns how to use words to achieve his aims and is therefore not a victim of language.
   (C) There is no consistent data to support whether language manipulates or is manipulated by an individual.
   (D) Childhood years are critical for verbal manipulation.
   (E) The degree to which language effects change in an individual is linked to the scope of the person's untapped imagination.

5. The central focus in Passage 1 is the
   (A) debate between two contradictory theories
   (B) child behavioral psychologist
   (C) purpose of language
   (D) young child
   (E) criminal

6. In Passage 2, what is the author's main objective?
   (A) to urge linguists and behaviorists to more carefully document their findings
   (B) to challenge the role language plays in communication
   (C) to seek harmony with and compassion for others
   (D) to belittle the masses to satisfy a select group
   (E) to dispute the need for theories explaining variations in communication

7. In the context of Passage **2**, what does "lauded" (line 53) most closely mean?
   (A) tolerated
   (B) praised
   (C) looked at suspiciously
   (D) condemned
   (E) made fun of

8. According to the author of Passage **2**, why might Americans be looked upon as "cretins" (line 63)?
   (A) They cannot protect themselves against the harsh cold climates of the North.
   (B) They refuse to acknowledge the universal value of snow in the verbal context of communication.
   (C) They do not comprehend the significance of snow in the culture of the Eskimo.
   (D) They are unwilling to recognize the diversity of snow in Alaska.
   (E) They are unable to verbally distinguish amongst various types of snow.

9. With which lines would both authors strongly agree?
   I.   "The ultimate use of...words is to affect one's environment to gain whatever the individual seeks." (Passage **1**, lines 37-38)
   II. "There is...something inherently wrong with language." (Passage **2**, line 50)
   III. "There is no evidence to indicate that the language one uses reflects a greater awareness of the world around him, or within him." (Passage **2**, lines 65-66)

   (A) I only
   (B) II only
   (C) I and III
   (D) II and III
   (E) I, II and III

10. In Passage **2**, how would one best describe the attitude the author has in the comments "though I'm sure there are one or two afterlife-linguists around..." (lines 68-69) and "If we were to smash a hammer..." (lines 73-74)?
    (A) tongue-in-cheek
    (B) frustrated
    (C) argumentative
    (D) deeply philosophical
    (E) melancholy

11. Which of the following reasons would best justify the author's concluding Passage *2* with the monosyllabically-rich phrase "the world would be a better place in which to live" (line 81)?

(A) The simple conclusion reinforces his view that important ideas can be stated without verbal extravagance.

(B) The simple words subtly ridicule those who expected a more elaborate, detailed and forceful concluding illustration.

(C) The word's ambivalent tone denies linguists the opportunity to claim that the author has himself become a victim of his own elaborate writing style.

(D) The concise conclusion avoids prolonging the argument through additional variables and considerations.

(E) The final thought hopes to seek compromise between those who support "white-collar" linguistics in America and those who wish to restore equality in the English language.

12. Which of the following is evident in one passage but lacking in the other?

    I. sentences posed as questions
    II. specific references to experts in the field
    III. facetious or mocking comments

(A) I only
(B) II only
(C) I and II
(D) II and III
(E) I, II and III

13. Which of the following most accurately compares/contrasts the attitudes of the

author of Passage *1* and *2*, respectively, toward the role language plays in a person's life?

(A) The former appreciates the variety of roles; the latter disputes any role that language plays.

(B) The former views it as a dynamic issue; the latter sees such discussions as sidestepping more critical issues.

(C) The former sees the role as a static entity; the latter views it as a tool of the wealthy.

(D) The former views language roles as mysterious and inconsistent; the latter finds language to be a contributing factor to unrest and disharmony.

(E) The former gives little credence to language as a viable tool; the latter views it as a necessity for social mobility.

The following information is for your reference - *it is provided on every SAT*

A circle measures 360°
A straight line measures 180°
The sum of the angles of a triangle is always 180°

Definition of symbols:
= *equal to*
≠ *not equal to*
< *less than*
> *greater than*
≤ *less than or equal to*
≥ *more than or equal to*
‖ *parallel to*
⊥ *perpendicular to*

all numbers used are real numbers

FORMULAS

Circle

$A = \pi r^2$
$C = 2\pi r$

Rectangle

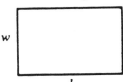

$A = lw$

Triangle

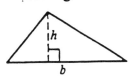

$A = 1/2 bh$

Rectangular prism

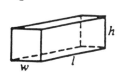

$V = lwh$

Cylinder

$V = \pi r^2 h$

Right triangle

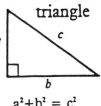

$a^2 + b^2 = c^2$
(Pythagorean Formula)

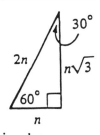

Special Right Triangles

SECTION 6
MATHEMATICS
15 minutes - 10 questions
MULTIPLE CHOICE PROBLEMS

1. If Pearl borrowed $20,000 from a bank charging 8% annual simple interest for the one-year loan, how much would she need to pay back at the end of the year?
   (A) $16,000
   (B) $21,600
   (C) $22,500
   (D) $28,000
   (E) $36,000

2.

note: **figure not drawn to scale**

$x+y =$
   (A) 30
   (B) 60
   (C) 90
   (D) 120
   (E) there is not enough information given

3. When converted to a fraction,
   $28\frac{4}{7}\% =$
   (A) 4/7
   (B) 1/4
   (C) 3/8
   (D) 2/7
   (E) 2/9

4. Team **A** has 4 players whose average height is 5 ft. 8 in. How tall would a new teammate need to be to bring the team's average height up to exactly 6 feet?
   (A) 7 ft. 4 in.
   (B) 6 ft. 8 in.
   (C) 6 ft. 6 in.
   (D) 6 ft. 4 in.
   (E) 6 ft. 2 in.

5. $(x + 2y)^2 - (x - 2y)^2 =$
   (A) 0
   (B) 8xy
   (C) $8y^2$
   (D) $2x^2 + 4y$
   (E) $3(x+2y)^2$

6.

If the cube pictured above is cut into three equal pieces, what is the ratio of the volume of one of these pieces to the sum of the volumes of the other two?
   (A) 1:2
   (B) 1:3
   (C) 1:9
   (D) 1:18
   (E) 1:27

7. For which value of **a** is $\dfrac{a^2 \cdot a^8}{a^5} = a^3$

    I.   -1
    II. 0
    III. 1

(A) I only
(B) II only
(C) III only
(D) I and III
(E) I, II and III

9. $3^5 + 3^6 =$
(A) $3^7 + 3^4$
(B) 3^{11}
(C) $2(3^6 - 3^5)$
(D) $5(3^4) + 6(3^5)$
(E) $3^{11} \div 3^4$

8. Stanley has $17 more than Mary and $13 more than Bert. If Stanley has $45 but wants everyone to have an equal amount of money, how much total money will he need to give to the other two?
(A) $3
(B) $5
(C) $7
(D) $10
(E) $20

10. A, B, C, D, E and F are points on a number line, in the order given. If $8AB = 4BD = 2AE = 6DF$, and $9AB = 4.5AC$, which of the following line segments is NOT equal in length to the others?
(A) AB
(B) BC
(C) CD
(D) DE
(E) EF

CHALLENGING SAT FINAL EXAM answers (level-numbers in parentheses*)

VERBAL Section 1	MATH Section 2	VERBAL Section 3	MATH Section 4	VERBAL Section 5	MATH Section 6
1. A (1)	1. A (1)	1. E (1)	1. B (1)	1. D (2)	1. B (1)
2. C (1)	2. E (1)	2. D (2)	2. C (1)	2. C (3)	2. C (3)
3. E (2)	3. C (1)	3. B (2)	3. B (2)	3. D (2)	3. E (2)
4. D (2)	4. B (2)	4. D (2)	4. D (2)	4. B (5)	4. A (4)
5. B (3)	5. B (2)	5. C (3)	5. C (3)	5. C (2)	5. B (3)
6. E (3)	6. D (2)	6. A (3)	6. D (3)	6. E (3)	6. A (3)
7. B (4)	7. A (3)	7. D (4)	7. B (2)	7. B (2)	7. D (4)
8. A (4)	8. B (2)	8. E (3)	8. A (3)	8. E (3)	8. D (4)
9. D (5)	9. E (3)	9. C (4)	9. C (3)	9. A (5)	9. C (4)
10. B (1)	10. E (3)	10. C (5)	10. B (3)	10. A (5)	10. E (5)
11. E (1)	11. A (2)	11. B (1)	11. D (3)	11. A (4)	
12. A (2)	12. D (2)	12. B (2)	12. A (3)	12. E (4)	
13. D (3)	13. B (3)	13. B (2)	13. A (4)	13. B (4)	
14. B (4)	14. E (4)	14. D (2)	14. C (3)		
15. C (5)	15. A (3)	15. E (3)	15. A (4)		
16. D (5)	16. C (4)	16. C (3)	16. 8.5 or 17/2 (2)		
17. D (2)	17. C (3)	17. D (4)	17. .215 (2)		
18. E (3)	18. D (3)	18. B (4)	18. 135 (2)		
19. B (1)	19. D (4)	19. A (3)	19. 3 (2)		
20. A (3)	20. B (4)	20. A (4)	20. 12 (3)		
21. C (2)	21. D (4)	21. E (4)	21. 7 (3)		
22. E (2)	22. E (5)	22. E (4)	22. 4/7 or .571 (3)		
23. C (2)	23. C (4)	23. A (5)	23. 7/13 or .538 (3)		
24. E (2)	24. C (4)	24. C (2)	24. 33.3 (4)		
25. A (3)	25. A (5)	25. B (3)	25. 240 (4)		
26. C (4)		26. C (4)			
27. D (4)		27. D (3)			
28. A (4)		28. B (3)			
29. B (2)		29. A (4)			
30. C (2)		30. A (3)			
		31. E (4)			
		32. D (2)			
		33. C (3)			
		34. E (4)			
		35. A (2)			

*Explanation of level-numbers:
    (1) easy; almost all students will get it correct
    (2) fairly easy; most students will get it correct
    (3) medium; approximately ½ will get it correct
    (4) difficult; not many students will get it correct
    (5) hard (for Math, oftentimes tricky); few students will get it correct

CHALLENGING SAT FINAL EXAM
WORKSHEET (to calculate your scores)
SAT-Verbal Sections

A. Section 1:   _____ - 1/4 x (_____)   =   _____
                      no. correct   no. incorrect   subtotal A

B. Section 3:   _____ - 1/4 x (_____)   =   _____
                      no. correct   no. incorrect   subtotal B

C. Section 5:   _____ - 1/4 x (_____)   =   _____
                      no. correct   no. incorrect   subtotal C

D. Total unrounded raw score
(add subtotals A-C)   _____

E. Total rounded raw score
(nearest whole number)   _____

F. SAT-verbal scaled score
(See the scoring chart on next page)

SAT-Mathematics Sections

A. Section 2:   _____ - 1/4 x (_____)   =   _____
                      no. correct   no. incorrect   subtotal A

B. Section 4:
Questions 1 through 15
(4-choice)   _____ - 1/3 x (_____)   =   _____
                      no. correct   no. incorrect   subtotal B

C. Section 4:
Questions 16 through 25
(Student Produced Answers)   _____   (no penalty for incorrect   =   _____
                      no. correct   answers on this section)   subtotal C

D. Section 6:   _____ - 1/4 x (_____)   =   _____
                      no. correct   no. incorrect   subtotal D

E. Total unrounded raw score
(add subtotals A-D)   _____

F. Total rounded raw score
(nearest whole number)   _____

G. SAT-mathematics scaled score
(See the scoring chart on next page)

VERBAL

MATH

Raw Score	Recentered Scale	Raw Score	Recentered Scale	Raw Score	Recentered Scale	Raw Score	Recentered Scale
78	800	35	510	60	800	25	480
77	800	34	500	59	800	24	470
76	800	33	500	58	790	23	470
		32	490	57	770	22	460
75	800	31	480	56	760	21	450
74	790						
73	780	30	480	55	740	20	440
72	760	29	470	54	730	19	430
71	750	28	460	53	720	18	430
		27	460	52	700	17	420
70	740	26	450	51	680	16	410
69	730						
68	720	25	440	50	670	15	410
67	710	24	440	49	660	14	400
66	700	23	430	48	650	13	390
		22	420	47	650	12	380
65	690	21	420	46	640	11	370
64	680						
63	680	20	410	45	640	10	360
62	670	19	400	44	630	9	350
61	660	18	400	43	620	8	340
		17	390	42	610	7	330
60	660	16	380	41	600	6	320
59	650						
58	650	15	370	40	600	5	310
57	640	14	370	39	590	4	300
56	630	13	360	38	580	3	290
		12	350	37	570	2	280
55	620	11	350	36	560	1	260
54	610						
53	600	10	340	35	560	0	240
52	600	9	330	34	550	-1	230
51	600	8	320	33	540	-2	220
		7	310	32	530	-3	210
50	590	6	300	31	520	-4	
49	590					or below	200
48	580	5	290	30	520		
47	580	4	280	29	510		
46	570	3	270	28	500		
		2	260	27	490		
45	570	1	250	26	480		
44	560						
43	560	0	240				
42	550	-1	230				
41	540	-2	220				
		-3	210				
40	540	-4					
39	530	or below	200				
38	530						
37	520						
36	510						

VERBAL

MATH

(a quick checklist to ensure that, after having taken the CHALLENGING SAT FINAL EXAM, you took the proper steps to ensure a MAXIMUM score)

Did you...

VERBAL	MATH
☐ Stay focused	☐ Stay focused
☐ Answer all questions	☐ Do the easy problems
☐ Use the limited-elimination strategy	☐ Work out each problem
☐ Allow sufficient time for READING	☐ Work carefully and avoid careless errors
☐ Use your finger for optimal speed/accuracy on the READING portion	☐ Avoid rushing
☐ Look for WRONG answers on the READING questions	☐ Recheck to be sure you answered the questions being asked
☐ Get the easy questions correct	☐ Avoid spending/wasting time on the harder problems

on Verbal : be aggressive

(allow <u>ample time</u> for READING protion!)

on MATH : be careful

(don't rush!)

If you are...	Verbal Advice

Getting too many SENTENCE COMPLETION problems wrong	• Focus on answering the easy ones; consider skipping the final two or three problems.
	
	• LONG TERM:
	    1) Practice
	    2) Build up vocabulary

Getting too many ANALOGIES problems wrong	• Practice and look over your errors; remember the relationship strategies. • LONG TERM: Build up vocabulary
Getting too many READING questions wrong	• Consider allowing more time for this portion. • Answer the easy questions first; skipping the more-complicated questions may not be a bad idea. • Look for the <u>wrong</u> answers and eliminate them.

Not comprehending the READING passage	• Follow the speed-reading finger-technique; underline phrases or sentences that contain main points (to help you better understand and be able to return to key parts in the passage).
	• Read the passage quickly to get a basic idea what it is about; then read more deeply where you need to (i.e., to answer specific questions). Note the author's <u>tone</u> and <u>main purpose</u> in the passage.
	
	• LONG TERM
	    1) Practice doing SAT reading passages
	    2) Do other focus-oriented activities (for example: crossword/logic puzzles)

Running out of time	• Work more quickly on the SENTENCE COMPLETIONS and ANALOGIES portions, allocating more time for the READING portion.

on VERBAL : be aggressive

(allow <u>ample time</u>
for READING portion!)

MATH

If you are...	**Math Advice**
Getting too many problems incorrect	• Do the ones you know, avoiding the final problems. • Work slowly and carefully; show your work to avoid making careless errors. • LONG TERM: Practice and review your mistakes
Getting too few problems correct	• Follow the same advice as mentioned above, but try to answer more problems; avoid the final problems (they are usually only answered correctly by SAT-Math veterans).

(don't rush!)

The Karelitz SAT Dictionary of One-Word Definitions ($12.95):

Hi-Lite Publishing Co.
P.O. Box 240161
Honolulu, HI 96824

The New SAT In Ten Easy Steps ($8.95):

Adams Media
260 Center Street
Holbrook, MA 02343

10 Real SATs ($17.95):

The College Board
45 Columbus Avenue
New York, N.Y. 10023

Thesaurus: *Rogets* or similar (pocketbook edition, words listed in <u>alphabetical</u> order) ($3.95-$12.95):

Available at all book stores

Penny Press Crossword Puzzles/Logic Puzzles Magazines ($1.99-$4.99):

Penny Press, Inc.
6 Prowitt Street
Norwalk, CT 06855

The New Millennium Power Dictionary (release-date: December, 2000) – 1200 pages, top 25,000 words + sentences for reference and lifetime vocabulary-building:

For free color flyer with complete info., write to:
Hi-Lite Publishing Co.
P.O. Box 240161
Honolulu, HI 96824

Video: 2-Hour **SAT**-review video with practice test & puzzles ($20.00):

Hi-Lite Publishing Co.
P.O. Box 240161
Honolulu, HI 96824

Computer Program: *Verbal/Math Vanquish*:

for more info., write to:
J. Bair
P.O. Box 203
Shelton, CT 06484

Words
most often
appearing on the

SAT

240 WORDS YOU NEED TO KNOW

ABATE	DIMINISH	BANEFUL	POISONOUS
ABHOR	HATE	BEGUILE	DECEIVE
ABOMINATE	HATE	BELLICOSE	QUARRELSOME
ABRIDGE	SHORTEN	BELLIGERENT	WARLIKE
ABSTAIN	REFRAIN	BOMBASTIC	BOASTFUL
ACCOLADE	AWARD	BRAZEN	SHAMELESS
ACME	SUMMIT	BROWBEAT	BULLY
ADAMANT	INSISTENT	BUTTRESS	SUPPORT
ADEPT	SKILLED	CALAMITOUS	CATASTROPHIC
ADMONISH	WARN	CANDID	HONEST
ADROIT	SKILLFUL	CAPRICIOUS	CHANGEABLE
ADVERSITY	MISFORTUNE	CEDE	FORFEIT
AESTHETIC	ARTISTIC	CHASTISE	PUNISH
AFFABLE	FRIENDLY	CHRONIC	CONTINUING
AGILE	NIMBLE	CLANDESTINE	SECRET
ALIENATE	ESTRANGE	COMPLACENT	CONTENTED
ALLAY	CALM	CONCILIATE	PACIFY
AMBIGUOUS	VAGUE	CONCISE	BRIEF
AMICABLE	FRIENDLY	CONDONE	PARDON
AMITY	FRIENDSHIP	CONVENE	ASSEMBLE
AMORPHOUS	SHAPELESS	CONVERGE	MEET
ANIMOSITY	HATRED	COPIOUS	PLENTIFUL
ANNEX	ADD	CORPULENT	FAT
APATHETIC	UNCARING	CORROBORATE	CONFIRM
APEX	PEAK	COVENANT	AGREEMENT
APPEASE	PACIFY	COVERT	SECRET
ARDUOUS	DIFFICULT	COVET	DESIRE
ARROGANT	SNOBBY	CRYPTIC	MYSTERIOUS
ASSAIL	ATTACK	CULPABLE	GUILTY
ASSENT	AGREE	CURTAIL	SHORTEN
ASTUTE	PERCEPTIVE	DAUNTLESS	BRAVE
ATROCIOUS	TERRIBLE	DEARTH	SCARCITY
ATYPICAL	ABNORMAL	DEFER	DELAY
AUDACIOUS	BOLD	DELIVERANCE	LIBERATION
AUGMENT	INCREASE	DELUGE	FLOOD
AUSPICIOUS	FAVORABLE	DEMURE	SHY
AVARICE	GREED	DEPLORE	REGRET
AVERT	PREVENT	DERIDE	RIDICULE
BALEFUL	THREATENING	DESOLATE	DESERTED
BANAL	UNORIGINAL	DESTITUTE	POOR

DETER	PREVENT	HARROWING	DISTRESSING
DEVIOUS	DECEITFUL	HAUGHTY	ARROGANT
DEVOUT	FAITHFUL	HINDER	PREVENT
DIDACTIC	INFORMATIONAL	HOMAGE	RESPECT
DIFFIDENT	SHY	HOSTILE	UNFRIENDLY
DIGRESS	STRAY	IMMUTABLE	UNCHANGEABLE
DILIGENT	HARDWORKING	IMPARTIAL	UNBIASED
DISHEVELED	UNTIDY	IMPEDE	HINDER
DISINTERESTED	IMPARTIAL	IMPLAUSIBLE	UNBELIEVABLE
DISPARAGE	BELITTLE	IMPOVERISHED	POOR
DOCILE	MANAGEABLE	IMPUDENT	RUDE
DOGMATIC	OPINIONATED	INANE	SILLY
DOLEFUL	SAD	INCESSANT	CONTINUAL
ECCENTRIC	ODD	INCLEMENT	STORMY
ELEGIAC	SORROWFUL	INDIFFERENT	UNCONCERNED
ENIGMA	MYSTERY	INDIGENT	POOR
ENTREAT	BEG	INFAMOUS	DISGRACEFUL
ERODE	DECAY	INFLAMMABLE	BURNABLE
ESTRANGE	SEPARATE	INIMICAL	HARMFUL
EULOGIZE	PRAISE	INKLING	HINT
EUPHONY	HARMONY	INNOCUOUS	HARMLESS
EXODUS	MIGRATION	INNOVATIVE	CREATIVE
EXTOL	PRAISE	INSOLENT	RUDE
EXTRANEOUS	IRRELEVANT	INTERMINABLE	ENDLESS
EXTRICATE	LIBERATE	INTIMIDATE	FRIGHTEN
EXTROVERTED	OUTGOING	INTREPID	FEARLESS
FAMISHED	HUNGRY	INUNDATE	FLOOD
FAWN	BOOTLICK	INVALUABLE	PRICELESS
FICKLE	CHANGEABLE	INVIGORATE	ENERGIZE
FORGO	RELINQUISH	IRATE	ANGRY
FORLORN	UNHAPPY	JEOPARDY	DANGER
FRAIL	FRAGILE	KEN	KNOWLEDGE
FRIVOLOUS	SILLY	LAMENT	MOURN
FRUGAL	THRIFTY	LAUD	PRAISE
GARRULOUS	TALKATIVE	LETHAL	DEADLY
GENIAL	PLEASANT	LETHARGIC	SLUGGISH
GERMANE	RELEVANT	LEVITY	HUMOR
GOAD	URGE	LOATHE	HATE
GREGARIOUS	SOCIABLE	LOQUACIOUS	TALKATIVE
GULLIBLE	OVERTRUSTING	LUCRATIVE	PROFITABLE

LUDICROUS	ABSURD	SACCHARINE	SWEET
MALEVOLENT	EVIL	SAGE	WISE
MALICIOUS	SPITEFUL	SCOFF	MOCK
MEANDER	WANDER	SEDATE	CALM
MENACE	THREAT	SEDENTARY	INACTIVE
MENDACIOUS	FALSE	SERENITY	PEACE
METICULOUS	EXACT	SOVEREIGN	SUPREME
MIRTH	JOY	SPARTAN	DISCIPLINED
MOLLIFY	SOOTHE	SPRIGHTLY	LIVELY
NOMADIC	WANDERING	SPURIOUS	FALSE
NOVEL	NEW	SQUANDER	WASTE
NOXIOUS	HARMFUL	STALWART	COURAGEOUS
OBSCURE	UNCLEAR	STEALTHY	SNEAKY
OMINOUS	THREATENING	STRATAGEM	SCHEME
OSTRACIZE	EXCLUDE	SUCCUMB	SURRENDER
PACIFY	CALM	SUFFRAGE	VOTE
PALPABLE	EVIDENT	SUPERFICIAL	SHALLOW
PENURIOUS	STINGY	SUPERFLUOUS	UNNECESSARY
PITHY	CONCISE	TACITURN	RESERVED
PRAGMATIC	PRACTICAL	TANGIBLE	TOUCHABLE
PRECARIOUS	HAZARDOUS	TAUT	STRETCHED
PROCRASTINATE	DELAY	TENACIOUS	STEADFAST
PRODIGAL	WASTEFUL	TENUOUS	FLIMSY
PROFICIENT	SKILLFUL	TERSE	BRIEF
PROLIFIC	PRODUCTIVE	THWART	HINDER
PROSAIC	UNIMAGINATIVE	TIMOROUS	SHY
PROWESS	BRAVERY	TRANQUIL	PEACEFUL
PRUDENT	SENSIBLE	UNRULY	DISOBEDIENT
PUGNACIOUS	QUARRELSOME	VANQUISH	DEFEAT
QUELL	SUPPRESS	VERACIOUS	TRUTHFUL
RASH	RECKLESS	VIRTUOUS	HONORABLE
RATIFY	APPROVE	VIVACIOUS	LIVELY
RAVENOUS	HUNGRY	VOCIFEROUS	LOUD
RECLUSIVE	WITHDRAWN	WARY	CAUTIOUS
RELINQUISH	SURRENDER	WAYWARD	DISOBEDIENT
REPRIMAND	SCOLD	WHIMSICAL	IMPULSIVE
RETICENT	SHY	WILY	SLY
REVEL	DELIGHT	WRATH	ANGER
RIFE	ABUNDANT	ZANY	SILLY
RUE	REGRET	ZENITH	PEAK

to test you on your knowledge of the *240 Words You Need to Know:*

QUIZ DIRECTIONS: Circle the choice that is synonymous with the word in CAPITAL letters. (Time: allow 10 minutes per page)

ABATE	1. hesitate	2. reveal	3. diminish
ABHOR	1. hate	2. prevent	3. frighten
ABOMINATE	1. destroy	2. hate	3. punish
ABRIDGE	1. shorten	2. request	3. connect
ABSTAIN	1. abolish	2. damage	3. refrain
ACCOLADE	1. award	2. remedy	3. conspiracy
ACME	1. irritation	2. summit	3. dilemma
ADAMANT	1. brief	2. hilarious	3. insistent
ADEPT	1. durable	2. skilled	3. corrupt
ADMONISH	1. decrease	2. warn	3. arrange
ADROIT	1. abnormal	2. peaceful	3. skillful
ADVERSITY	1. misfortune	2. freedom	3. publicity
AESTHETIC	1. bitter	2. artistic	3. unfamiliar
AFFABLE	1. artificial	2. amazing	3. friendly
AGILE	1. breakable	2. nimble	3. lenient
ALIENATE	1. befriend	2. wander	3. estrange
ALLAY	1. delay	2. calm	3. magnify
AMBIGUOUS	1. colossal	2. vague	3. ridiculous
AMICABLE	1. skeptical	2. secretive	3. friendly
AMITY	1. friendship	2. rivalry	3. catastrophe
AMORPHOUS	1. shapeless	2. unnecessary	3. loving
ANIMOSITY	1. kinship	2. hatred	3. freedom
ANNEX	1. add	2. oppose	3. surrender
APATHETIC	1. uncaring	2. harmful	3. amusing
APEX	1. peak	2. argument	3. flaw
APPEASE	1. congratulate	2. appear	3. pacify
ARDUOUS	1. lively	2. important	3. difficult
ARROGANT	1. snobby	2. stubborn	3. zany
ASSAIL	1. attack	2. journey	3. prevent
ASSENT	1. deceive	2. agree	3. dominate
ASTUTE	1. clumsy	2. perceptive	3. fearless
ATROCIOUS	1. suspicious	2. talented	3. terrible
ATYPICAL	1. stylish	2. cautious	3. abnormal
AUDACIOUS	1. conceited	2. infamous	3. bold
AUGMENT	1. increase	2. insist	3. repeat
AUSPICIOUS	1. suspicious	2. favorable	3. disastrous
AVARICE	1. wealth	2. greed	3. authority
AVERT	1. fortify	2. slander	3. prevent
BALEFUL	1. threatening	2. luxurious	3. sad
BANAL	1. unoriginal	2. restrictive	3. sincere

BANEFUL	1. generous	2. logical	3. poisonous
BEGUILE	1. deceive	2. urge	3. inspire
BELLICOSE	1. enormous	2. quarrelsome	3. colorful
BELLIGERENT	1. picturesque	2. hesitant	3. warlike
BOMBASTIC	1. harmful	2. foul	3. boastful
BRAZEN	1. shameless	2. exotic	3. hazardous
BROWBEAT	1. guide	2. conquer	3. bully
BUTTRESS	1. support	2. expel	3. object
CALAMITOUS	1. persuasive	2. excessive	3. catastrophic
CANDID	1. secretive	2. persistent	3. honest
CAPRICIOUS	1. spacious	2. changeable	3. swift
CEDE	1. forfeit	2. nourish	3. protect
CHASTISE	1. cleanse	2. punish	3. pursue
CHRONIC	1. continuing	2. intricate	3. obsolete
CLANDESTINE	1. secret	2. inevitable	3. loyal
COMPLACENT	1. cooperative	2. sneaky	3. contented
CONCILIATE	1. pacify	2. disagree	3. comprehend
CONCISE	1. brief	2. large	3. practical
CONDONE	1. present	2. prevent	3. pardon
CONVENE	1. scheme	2. assemble	3. compare
CONVERGE	1. deceive	2. stray	3. meet
COPIOUS	1. repetitious	2. plentiful	3. forceful
CORPULENT	1. dead	2. tasty	3. fat
CORROBORATE	1. humiliate	2. confirm	3. decay
COVENANT	1. disguise	2. meeting	3. agreement
COVERT	1. secret	2. aware	3. sudden
COVET	1. shelter	2. desire	3. restore
CRYPTIC	1. deadly	2. mysterious	3. ancient
CULPABLE	1. foolish	2. guilty	3. correctable
CURTAIL	1. pursue	2. threaten	3. shorten
DAUNTLESS	1. worthless	2. unexpected	3. brave
DEARTH	1. scarcity	2. demise	3. pinnacle
DEFER	1. delay	2. respect	3. consult
DELIVERANCE	1. arrival	2. liberation	3. tolerance
DELUGE	1. flood	2. misunderstanding	3. separation
DEMURE	1. soft	2. showy	3. shy
DEPLORE	1. examine	2. regret	3. crave
DERIDE	1. ridicule	2. accompany	3. distribute
DESOLATE	1. unclear	2. deserted	3. sacred
DESTITUTE	1. confused	2. poor	3. unwavering

DETER	1. ramble	2. prevent	3. comprehend
DEVIOUS	1. deceitful	2. jealous	3. ingenious
DEVOUT	1. faithful	2. hungry	3. talkative
DIDACTIC	1. inactive	2. concluding	3. informational
DIFFIDENT	1. disagreeable	2. loyal	3. shy
DIGRESS	1. renew	2. stray	3. reread
DILIGENT	1. restless	2. obedient	3. hardworking
DISHEVELED	1. untidy	2. witty	3. concise
DISINTERESTED	1. impartial	2. tedious	3. unsupportive
DISPARAGE	1. exhibit	2. belittle	3. squander
DOCILE	1. calculating	2. manageable	3. shapeless
DOGMATIC	1. childish	2. opinionated	3. unplanned
DOLEFUL	1. confident	2. sad	3. generous
ECCENTRIC	1. circular	2. odd	3. unnecessary
ELEGIAC	1. sorrowful	2. jubilant	3. sluggish
ENIGMA	1. mystery	2. belief	3. display
ENTREAT	1. energize	2. feed	3. beg
ERODE	1. exterminate	2. decay	3. journey
ESTRANGE	1. separate	2. explore	3. establish
EULOGIZE	1. protest	2. praise	3. apologize
EUPHONY	1. harmony	2. imitation	3. joy
EXODUS	1. migration	2. revelation	3. brilliance
EXTOL	1. advance	2. escape	3. praise
EXTRANEOUS	1. irrelevant	2. unusual	3. strenuous
EXTRICATE	1. duplicate	2. liberate	3. simplify
EXTROVERTED	1. clever	2. abnormal	3. outgoing
FAMISHED	1. sociable	2. hungry	3. excited
FAWN	1. subdue	2. revel	3. bootlick
FICKLE	1. changeable	2. charming	3. humble
FORGO	1. fortify	2. relinquish	3. persevere
FORLORN	1. courteous	2. shy	3. unhappy
FRAIL	1. fragile	2. cruel	3. restless
FRIVOLOUS	1. tattered	2. intense	3. silly
FRUGAL	1. friendly	2. thrifty	3. lush
GARRULOUS	1. talkative	2. restless	3. mischievous
GENIAL	1. inherited	2. unimportant	3. pleasant
GERMANE	1. elaborate	2. relevant	3. harmful
GOAD	1. praise	2. burden	3. urge
GREGARIOUS	1. invincible	2. sociable	3. warlike
GULLIBLE	1. inventive	2. overtrusting	3. neglectful

HARROWING	1. abrupt	2. demanding	3. distressing
HAUGHTY	1. arrogant	2. bashful	3. mischievous
HINDER	1. pursue	2. condemn	3. prevent
HOMAGE	1. pride	2. respect	3. indifference
HOSTILE	1. unfriendly	2. comfortable	3. roaming
IMMUTABLE	1. infinite	2. unchangeable	3. deaf
IMPARTIAL	1. unfavorable	2. unbiased	3. complete
IMPEDE	1. hinder	2. annoy	3. wander
IMPLAUSIBLE	1. inexcusable	2. unbelievable	3. unpredictable
IMPOVERISHED	1. poor	2. outgoing	3. unethical
IMPUDENT	1. fearless	2. rude	3. unwise
INANE	1. silly	2. noisy	3. illegal
INCESSANT	1. unattractive	2. commonplace	3. continual
INCLEMENT	1. stormy	2. ambiguous	3. steep
INDIFFERENT	1. similar	2. rare	3. unconcerned
INDIGENT	1. poor	2. sociable	3. complete
INFAMOUS	1. honorable	2. anonymous	3. disgraceful
INFLAMMABLE	1. durable	2. sizable	3. burnable
INIMICAL	1. mysterious	2. ideal	3. harmful
INKLING	1. hint	2. disciple	3. blemish
INNOCUOUS	1. harmless	2. unpleasant	3. unwise
INNOVATIVE	1. defective	2. creative	3. stubborn
INSOLENT	1. warm	2. rude	3. united
INTERMINABLE	1. intermediate	2. incomplete	3. endless
INTIMIDATE	1. frighten	2. amuse	3. decrease
INTREPID	1. clumsy	2. clever	3. fearless
INUNDATE	1. protest	2. flood	3. disorganize
INVALUABLE	1. worthless	2. priceless	3. unavailable
INVIGORATE	1. introduce	2. complicate	3. energize
IRATE	1. confident	2. foolish	3. angry
JEOPARDY	1. freedom	2. trivia	3. danger
KEN	1. knowledge	2. friends	3. ambition
LAMENT	1. activate	2. mourn	3. explain
LAUD	1. yell	2. praise	3. criticize
LETHAL	1. deadly	2. permissible	3. amazing
LETHARGIC	1. cautious	2. timid	3. sluggish
LEVITY	1. humor	2. chaos	3. humbleness
LOATHE	1. comfort	2. succeed	3. hate
LOQUACIOUS	1. fussy	2. talkative	3. deceptive
LUCRATIVE	1. profitable	2. legitimate	3. pleasant

LUDICROUS	1. delicious	2. absurd	3. serious
MALEVOLENT	1. powerful	2. impartial	3. evil
MALICIOUS	1. fragrant	2. careless	3. spiteful
MEANDER	1. wander	2. complain	3. anger
MENACE	1. gathering	2. threat	3. dilemma
MENDACIOUS	1. correctable	2. false	3. obvious
METICULOUS	1. exact	2. inquisitive	3. stingy
MIRTH	1. tension	2. joy	3. curiosity
MOLLIFY	1. soothe	2. obey	3. scold
NOMADIC	1. furious	2. wandering	3. anonymous
NOVEL	1. long	2. absurd	3. new
NOXIOUS	1. fragrant	2. appropriate	3. harmful
OBSCURE	1. unclear	2. stubborn	3. sudden
OMINOUS	1. knowledgeable	2. fortunate	3. threatening
OSTRACIZE	1. analyze	2. realize	3. exclude
PACIFY	1. permit	2. calm	3. condense
PALPABLE	1. numerous	2. united	3. evident
PENURIOUS	1. stingy	2. scholarly	3. devoted
PITHY	1. temporary	2. absurd	3. concise
PRAGMATIC	1. intolerant	2. independent	3. practical
PRECARIOUS	1. premature	2. affectionate	3. hazardous
PROCRASTINATE	1. repeat	2. delay	3. denounce
PRODIGAL	1. urgent	2. amazing	3. wasteful
PROFICIENT	1. skillful	2. prompt	3. satisfactory
PROLIFIC	1. productive	2. talkative	3. wise
PROSAIC	1. diverse	2. unimaginative	3. poetic
PROWESS	1. abundance	2. bravery	3. mischief
PRUDENT	1. polite	2. restless	3. sensible
PUGNACIOUS	1. quarrelsome	2. tiny	3. witty
QUELL	1. strengthen	2. suppress	3. flood
RASH	1. reckless	2. endless	3. fearless
RATIFY	1. challenge	2. approve	3. reveal
RAVENOUS	1. hungry	2. furious	3. supreme
RECLUSIVE	1. negligent	2. admired	3. withdrawn
RELINQUISH	1. surrender	2. assist	3. destroy
REPRIMAND	1. restore	2. scold	3. manage
RETICENT	1. aware	2. informal	3. shy
REVEL	1. delight	2. uncover	3. refrain
RIFE	1. abundant	2. ominous	3. mature
RUE	1. avoid	2. regret	3. urge

SACCHARINE	1. artificial	2. sweet	3. dry
SAGE	1. flimsy	2. ancient	3. wise
SCOFF	1. mock	2. hurry	3. discipline
SEDATE	1. secretive	2. authoritative	3. calm
SEDENTARY	1. inactive	2. firm	3. bashful
SERENITY	1. strength	2. peace	3. friendship
SOVEREIGN	1. foreign	2. boring	3. supreme
SPARTAN	1. extravagant	2. competitive	3. disciplined
SPRIGHTLY	1. precise	2. lively	3. silly
SPURIOUS	1. angry	2. false	3. harmful
SQUANDER	1. crush	2. separate	3. waste
STALWART	1. sly	2. courageous	3. pessimistic
STEALTHY	1. corrupt	2. sneaky	3. cheerful
STRATAGEM	1. scheme	2. opponent	3. discovery
SUCCUMB	1. surrender	2. complain	3. flatter
SUFFRAGE	1. vote	2. protection	3. distress
SUPERFICIAL	1. shallow	2. extraordinary	3. organized
SUPERFLUOUS	1. magnificent	2. unnecessary	3. tranquil
TACITURN	1. nervous	2. polite	3. reserved
TANGIBLE	1. touchable	2. tasty	3. fragile
TAUT	1. flashy	2. stretched	3. stormy
TENACIOUS	1. lethargic	2. muscular	3. steadfast
TENUOUS	1. flimsy	2. sensible	3. shocking
TERSE	1. creative	2. flexible	3. brief
THWART	1. hinder	2. punish	3. exaggerate
TIMOROUS	1. shy	2. excited	3. romantic
TRANQUIL	1. temporary	2. peaceful	3. sturdy
UNRULY	1. exceptional	2. disobedient	3. inflexible
VANQUISH	1. defeat	2. manage	3. protest
VERACIOUS	1. destructive	2. truthful	3. hungry
VIRTUOUS	1. unrealistic	2. accurate	3. honorable
VIVACIOUS	1. greedy	2. rebellious	3. lively
VOCIFEROUS	1. childish	2. loud	3. nervous
WARY	1. candid	2. cautious	3. hostile
WAYWARD	1. loyal	2. adventurous	3. disobedient
WHIMSICAL	1. impulsive	2. melodious	3. sensible
WILY	1. determined	2. cheerful	3. sly
WRATH	1. confusion	2. leisure	3. anger
ZANY	1. silly	2. sloppy	3. shocking
ZENITH	1. peak	2. tranquillity	3. humor

[note: Permission is given to make copies of this page, for quiz-taking and highlighting/reviewing unfamiliar words.]

240 WORDS YOU OUGHT TO KNOW

ABEYANCE	INACTIVITY	CONSECRATE	DEDICATE
ABSTEMIOUS	MODERATE	CONSTERNATION	AMAZEMENT
ACQUIESCE	CONSENT	CONTUMACIOUS	DISOBEDIENT
ACRIMONIOUS	RESENTFUL	CRAVEN	COWARDLY
ACUMEN	KEENNESS	CREDULOUS	GULLIBLE
AGGRANDIZE	EXALT	CUPIDITY	DESIRE
ALACRITY	PROMPTNESS	CURSORY	HASTY
ALTERCATION	QUARREL	DEBILITATE	WEAKEN
AMELIORATE	IMPROVE	DECOROUS	PROPER
ANATHEMA	CURSE	DECRY	CRITICIZE
ANIMADVERSION	CRITICISM	DEFERENCE	RESPECT
APOCRYPHAL	FALSE	DELETERIOUS	HARMFUL
APOGEE	ZENITH	DEMUR	OBJECT
APOLOGIST	DEFENDER	DERISIVE	SCORNFUL
APOSTATE	DESERTER	DESCRY	OBSERVE
APOTHEOSIS	GLORIFICATION	DESICCATE	DRY
ASCETIC	AUSTERE	DESULTORY	AIMLESS
ASSIDUOUS	DETERMINED	DIFFUSE	WORDY
ASSUAGE	EASE	DILATORY	DELAYING
ATROPHY	DETERIORATION	DISCURSIVE	RAMBLING
AUGUR	PREDICT	DISINGENUOUS	INSINCERE
AUGUST	NOBLE	DISPUTATIOUS	ARGUMENTATIVE
AUSTERE	STRICT	DISSIMULATE	PRETEND
AVERSION	DISLIKE	DISSIPATE	SCATTER
BACCHANALIAN	DRUNKEN	DISSOLUTE	IMMORAL
BLITHE	HAPPY	DUPLICITY	DECEIT
CALLOW	NAÏVE	ECLAT	SPLENDOR
CALUMNIATE	SLANDER	ECLECTIC	DIVERSE
CANARD	HOAX	EDIFY	INSTRUCT
CAPACIOUS	SPACIOUS	EFFERVESCENT	EXCITED
CASTIGATE	REPRIMAND	EFFRONTERY	SHAMELESSNESS
CAVIL	COMPLAIN	EGREGIOUS	FLAGRANT
CELERITY	SWIFTNESS	ELEEMOSYNARY	CHARITABLE
CHAGRIN	FRUSTRATION	ENCOMIUM	PRAISE
CHARLATAN	FRAUD	ENERVATE	WEAKEN
CHARY	CAUTIOUS	ENNUI	BOREDOM
CHICANERY	TRICKERY	EPHEMERAL	BRIEF
CIRCUITOUS	ROUNDABOUT	EQUANIMITY	COMPOSURE
COMPUNCTION	UNEASINESS	EQUIVOCAL	AMBIGUOUS
CONCATENATE	LINK	ERUDITE	SCHOLARLY

ESCHEW	AVOID	INDOLENT	LAZY
ETHEREAL	DELICATE	INEXORABLE	RELENTLESS
EUPHONIOUS	HARMONIOUS	INSIDIOUS	DEVIOUS
EXECRABLE	ABOMINABLE	INSIPID	UNINTERESTING
EXHORT	ENCOURAGE	INSOUCIANT	CAREFREE
EXIGUOUS	SCANTY	INTRACTABLE	STUBBORN
EXORCISE	EXPEL	INTRANSIGENT	STUBBORN
EXTIRPATE	DESTROY	INVEIGH	DENOUNCE
FACETIOUS	SILLY	INVIDIOUS	INSULTING
FACTIOUS	QUARRELSOME	JEJUNE	IMMATURE
FACTITIOUS	ARTIFICIAL	JOCOSE	JOKING
FALLOW	UNDEVELOPED	LABYRINTHINE	INTRICATE
FATUOUS	FOOLISH	LACHRYMOSE	CRYING
FECUND	FERTILE	LACONIC	CONCISE
FEIGN	PRETEND	LANGUID	SLUGGISH
FLACCID	FLABBY	LASSITUDE	WEARINESS
FLAGITIOUS	WICKED	LIMPID	CLEAR
FLIPPANT	DISRESPECTFUL	LITHE	GRACEFUL
FORBEARANCE	PATIENCE	LUGUBRIOUS	GLOOMY
FRACTIOUS	UNRULY	MACHIAVELLIAN	DEVIOUS
FRENETIC	FRANTIC	MINUTIAE	TRIVIA
FURTIVE	SNEAKY	MISCREANT	VILLAIN
GALVANIZE	AROUSE	MITIGATE	LESSEN
GAUNT	BONY	MORDANT	SARCASTIC
GOSSAMER	DELICATE	MOUNTEBANK	FRAUD
HACKNEYED	OVERUSED	NEFARIOUS	EVIL
HALCYON	PEACEFUL	NONCHALANT	UNCONCERNED
HEDONISTIC	PLEASUREFUL	OBFUSCATE	CONFUSE
HEINOUS	HORRIBLE	OBLOQUY	SHAME
IGNOBLE	SHAMEFUL	OBSEQUIOUS	SERVILE
IGNOMINIOUS	SHAMEFUL	OBSTREPEROUS	UNRULY
IMPECCABLE	FLAWLESS	OFFICIOUS	INTERFERING
IMPECUNIOUS	POOR	ONEROUS	BURDENSOME
IMPERIOUS	DOMINEERING	OPULENT	WEALTHY
IMPORTUNE	BEG	OSTENSIBLE	APPARENT
IMPUGN	ATTACK	OSTENTATIOUS	SHOWY
INCOMMENSURATE	INADEQUATE	PAEAN	PRAISE
INCULCATE	TEACH	PALLIATE	RELIEVE
INCULPATE	ACCUSE	PANACEA	REMEDY
INDIGENOUS	NATIVE	PANEGYRIC	EULOGY

PARIAH	OUTCAST	SOMNOLENT	SLEEPY
PARSIMONIOUS	STINGY	SOPHOMORIC	IMMATURE
PAUCITY	SCARCITY	SOPORIFIC	SLEEPY
PENCHANT	LIKING	SPECIOUS	DECEPTIVE
PERCIPIENT	PERCEPTIVE	SPLENETIC	IRRITABLE
PERFIDIOUS	DISLOYAL	SPORTIVE	PLAYFUL
PERFUNCTORY	UNENTHUSIASTIC	SQUALID	FILTHY
PERSPICACIOUS	PERCEPTIVE	STENTORIAN	THUNDEROUS
PLAINTIVE	MOURNFUL	STRIDENT	HARSH
PRECIPITOUS	STEEP	SUCCINCT	CONCISE
PRECOCIOUS	ADVANCED	SUPERCILIOUS	ARROGANT
PREDILECTION	PREFERENCE	SUPPLICATE	BEG
PROBITY	HONESTY	SURFEIT	SURPLUS
PRODIGIOUS	ENORMOUS	SURLY	GROUCHY
PROFLIGATE	WASTEFUL	SURREPTITIOUS	SECRETIVE
PROLIX	WORDY	SYCOPHANT	FLATTERER
PROPINQUITY	NEARNESS	SYLVAN	WOODED
PROPITIATE	APPEASE	TIRADE	REPRIMAND
PUERILE	CHILDISH	TOADY	FLATTERER
PULCHRITUDE	BEAUTY	TORPID	SLUGGISH
PURITANICAL	STRICT	TRANSITORY	TEMPORARY
PUSILLANIMOUS	COWARDLY	TRUCULENT	BELLIGERENT
QUANDARY	DILEMMA	TRUNCATE	SHORTEN
QUERULOUS	COMPLAINING	TUMID	SWOLLEN
QUIESCENT	INACTIVE	TURBID	MUDDY
QUIXOTIC	IDEALISTIC	TURGID	SWOLLEN
RAPACIOUS	GREEDY	UBIQUITOUS	EVERYWHERE
RECALCITRANT	STUBBORN	UPBRAID	SCOLD
RECTITUDE	HONOR	VENERATE	WORSHIP
REPINE	COMPLAIN	VERBOSE	WORDY
REPUDIATE	REJECT	VERDANT	LUSH
RESPITE	PAUSE	VERITABLE	ACTUAL
RESTIVE	RESTLESS	VICARIOUS	INDIRECT
SACROSANCT	SACRED	VILIFY	SLANDER
SAGACIOUS	WISE	VIRULENT	POISONOUS
SALUBRIOUS	HEALTHFUL	VITRIOLIC	SARCASTIC
SATIATE	SATISFY	VOLUBLE	TALKATIVE
SATURNINE	GLOOMY	VORACIOUS	RAVENOUS
SEDULOUS	DILIGENT	WINSOME	CHARMING
SOLICITUDE	CONCERN	WIZENED	SHRIVELED

to test you on your knowledge of the *240 Words You Ought to Know:*

ABEYANCE	1. obedience	2. denial	3. inactivity
ABSTEMIOUS	1. scornful	2. moderate	3. boastful
ACQUIESCE	1. consent	2. acquire	3. accompany
ACRIMONIOUS	1. unaware	2. resentful	3. hospitable
ACUMEN	1. keenness	2. dislike	3. friendship
AGGRANDIZE	1. exalt	2. accumulate	3. befriend
ALACRITY	1. promptness	2. normalcy	3. poverty
ALTERCATION	1. improvement	2. modification	3. quarrel
AMELIORATE	1. melt	2. improve	3. antagonize
ANATHEMA	1. curse	2. remedy	3. hymn
ANIMADVERSION	1. liveliness	2. love	3. criticism
APOCRYPHAL	1. futuristic	2. perplexing	3. false
APOGEE	1. sincerity	2. leisure	3. zenith
APOLOGIST	1. defender	2. pioneer	3. moron
APOSTATE	1. leader	2. deserter	3. disciple
APOTHEOSIS	1. glorification	2. anticlimax	3. theory
ASCETIC	1. bitter	2. austere	3. prosperous
ASSIDUOUS	1. harsh	2. skeptical	3. determined
ASSUAGE	1. ease	2. amaze	3. despise
ATROPHY	1. praise	2. deterioration	3. pity
AUGUR	1. allow	2. predict	3. restrict
AUGUST	1. arrogant	2. noble	3. submissive
AUSTERE	1. clever	2. silly	3. strict
AVERSION	1. compassion	2. perseverence	3. dislike
BACCHANALIAN	1. elaborate	2. organized	3. drunken
BLITHE	1. heavy	2. sharp	3. happy
CALLOW	1. daring	2. naive	3. popular
CALUMNIATE	1. trespass	2. slander	3. evaluate
CANARD	1. prevention	2. desire	3. hoax
CAPACIOUS	1. false	2. spacious	3. powerful
CASTIGATE	1. burden	2. celebrate	3. reprimand
CAVIL	1. complain	2. strike	3. warn
CELERITY	1. swiftness	2. fame	3. pleasance
CHAGRIN	1. frustration	2. amusement	3. difficulty
CHARLATAN	1. emperor	2. idealist	3. fraud
CHARY	1. inactive	2. cautious	3. naive
CHICANERY	1. ethnicity	2. cowardice	3. trickery
CIRCUITOUS	1. fundamental	2. roundabout	3. attractive
COMPUNCTION	1. uneasiness	2. promptness	3. honesty
CONCATENATE	1. link	2. disregard	3. demolish

CONSECRATE	1. accelerate	2. dedicate	3. converge
CONSTERNATION	1. amazement	2. adventure	3. disagreement
CONTUMACIOUS	1. carefree	2. disobedient	3. greedy
CRAVEN	1. desirous	2. independent	3. cowardly
CREDULOUS	1. dishonorable	2. melancholy	3. gullible
CUPIDITY	1. clumsiness	2. desire	3. tenderness
CURSORY	1. hasty	2. angry	3. unique
DEBILITATE	1. weaken	2. expand	3. simplify
DECOROUS	1. proper	2. elaborate	3. logical
DECRY	1. boast	2. criticize	3. worry
DEFERENCE	1. endurance	2. respect	3. postponement
DELETERIOUS	1. essential	2. domineering	3. harmful
DEMUR	1. object	2. avoid	3. display
DERISIVE	1. perceptive	2. unoriginal	3. scornful
DESCRY	1. shout	2. observe	3. denounce
DESICCATE	1. dry	2. destroy	3. condemn
DESULTORY	1. aimless	2. sarcastic	3. disobedient
DIFFUSE	1. timid	2. dense	3. wordy
DILATORY	1. strengthening	2. delaying	3. accompanying
DISCURSIVE	1. amusing	2. rambling	3. furious
DISINGENUOUS	1. insincere	2. idiotic	3. unselfish
DISPUTATIOUS	1. gullible	2. nervous	3. argumentative
DISSIMULATE	1. originate	2. interrogate	3. pretend
DISSIPATE	1. await	2. scatter	3. pacify
DISSOLUTE	1. arrogant	2. immoral	3. diligent
DUPLICITY	1. deceit	2. simplicity	3. imitation
ECLAT	1. obstacle	2. distress	3. splendor
ECLECTIC	1. lively	2. diverse	3. religious
EDIFY	1. instruct	2. alter	3. slander
EFFERVESCENT	1. vague	2. excited	3. cautious
EFFRONTERY	1. poise	2. honesty	3. shamelessness
EGREGIOUS	1. glorious	2. authentic	3. flagrant
ELEEMOSYNARY	1. charitable	2. devoted	3. deceitful
ENCOMIUM	1. praise	2. decision	3. arrival
ENERVATE	1. stimulate	2. clarify	3. weaken
ENNUI	1. boredom	2. anger	3. thoughtfulness
EPHEMERAL	1. brief	2. fragile	3. eccentric
EQUANIMITY	1. excitement	2. composure	3. equality
EQUIVOCAL	1. loud	2. calm	3. ambiguous
ERUDITE	1. stylish	2. scholarly	3. impolite

ESCHEW	1. digest	2. avoid	3. accompany
ETHEREAL	1. delicate	2. fragrant	3. artistic
EUPHONIOUS	1. fraudulent	2. harmonious	3. thunderous
EXECRABLE	1. favorable	2. exceptional	3. abominable
EXHORT	1. encourage	2. defeat	3. exclude
EXIGUOUS	1. hasty	2. urgent	3. scanty
EXORCISE	1. strengthen	2. expel	3. practice
EXTIRPATE	1. alter	2. destroy	3. expand
FACETIOUS	1. silly	2. faithful	3. violent
FACTIOUS	1. actual	2. enthusiastic	3. quarrelsome
FACTITIOUS	1. absolute	2. artificial	3. debatable
FALLOW	1. undeveloped	2. sickly	3. continual
FATUOUS	1. obese	2. intolerant	3. foolish
FECUND	1. fertile	2. nonessential	3. foul
FEIGN	1. dominate	2. pretend	3. warn
FLACCID	1. flabby	2. bitter	3. transparent
FLAGITIOUS	1. loyal	2. wicked	3. ambitious
FLIPPANT	1. disrespectful	2. unaware	3. hesitant
FORBEARANCE	1. anticipation	2. bravery	3. patience
FRACTIOUS	1. incomplete	2. elderly	3. unruly
FRENETIC	1. amiable	2. frantic	3. resentful
FURTIVE	1. playful	2. restless	3. sneaky
GALVANIZE	1. arouse	2. speculate	3. separate
GAUNT	1. eerie	2. polite	3. bony
GOSSAMER	1. desolate	2. identical	3. delicate
HACKNEYED	1. overused	2. fragmented	3. novel
HALCYON	1. gigantic	2. peaceful	3. ancient
HEDONISTIC	1. pleasureful	2. skeptical	3. intellectual
HEINOUS	1. constant	2. horrible	3. noble
IGNOBLE	1. demanding	2. trustworthy	3. shameful
IGNOMINIOUS	1. shameful	2. dignified	3. tiny
IMPECCABLE	1. unruly	2. worthless	3. flawless
IMPECUNIOUS	1. eccentric	2. marvelous	3. poor
IMPERIOUS	1. domineering	2. wealthy	3. childish
IMPORTUNE	1. beg	2. accumulate	3. simplify
IMPUGN	1. annoy	2. attack	3. captivate
INCOMMENSURATE	1. inadequate	2. confused	3. unheralded
INCULCATE	1. deny	2. fatigue	3. teach
INCULPATE	1. depict	2. accuse	3. charm
INDIGENOUS	1. disloyal	2. native	3. unaware

INDOLENT	1. melancholy	2. lazy	3. vague
INEXORABLE	1. essential	2. inadequate	3. relentless
INSIDIOUS	1. comprehensive	2. envious	3. devious
INSIPID	1. clean	2. uninteresting	3. clever
INSOUCIANT	1. serene	2. unbearable	3. carefree
INTRACTABLE	1. stubborn	2. inevitable	3. clumsy
INTRANSIGENT	1. unclear	2. unfamiliar	3. stubborn
INVEIGH	1. denounce	2. condense	3. omit
INVIDIOUS	1. generous	2. productive	3. insulting
JEJUNE	1. nutritious	2. immature	3. durable
JOCOSE	1. nomadic	2. joking	3. indifferent
LABYRINTHINE	1. intricate	2. youthful	3. amiable
LACHRYMOSE	1. crying	2. indifferent	3. intricate
LACONIC	1. concise	2. complex	3. lethargic
LANGUID	1. scholarly	2. sluggish	3. bony
LASSITUDE	1. weariness	2. attractiveness	3. isolation
LIMPID	1. swollen	2. weak	3. clear
LITHE	1. talkative	2. graceful	3. sluggish
LUGUBRIOUS	1. gloomy	2. healthy	3. tedious
MACHIAVELLIAN	1. romantic	2. devious	3. noble
MINUTIAE	1. reduction	2. moment	3. trivia
MISCREANT	1. mutation	2. villain	3. laggard
MITIGATE	1. lessen	2. tease	3. clarify
MORDANT	1. helpful	2. sarcastic	3. incompetent
MOUNTEBANK	1. fraud	2. guard	3. barrier
NEFARIOUS	1. distant	2. royal	3. evil
NONCHALANT	1. unconcerned	2. skillful	3. ungrateful
OBFUSCATE	1. accumulate	2. condemn	3. confuse
OBLOQUY	1. greed	2. shame	3. conference
OBSEQUIOUS	1. rebellious	2. servile	3. sentimental
OBSTREPEROUS	1. elaborate	2. unruly	3. dilapidated
OFFICIOUS	1. studious	2. serious	3. interfering
ONEROUS	1. burdensome	2. lonely	3. dislikable
OPULENT	1. wealthy	2. bashful	3. arrogant
OSTENSIBLE	1. apparent	2. triumphant	3. sociable
OSTENTATIOUS	1. malicious	2. efficient	3. showy
PAEAN	1. idol	2. hazard	3. praise
PALLIATE	1. accomplish	2. depress	3. relieve
PANACEA	1. remedy	2. affliction	3. desire
PANEGYRIC	1. sharpness	2. vigilance	3. eulogy

PARIAH	1. outcast	2. priest	3. bystander
PARSIMONIOUS	1. religious	2. stingy	3. unemotional
PAUCITY	1. catastrophe	2. scarcity	3. patience
PENCHANT	1. salary	2. liking	3. summary
PERCIPIENT	1. perceptive	2. scornful	3. submissive
PERFIDIOUS	1. envious	2. persistent	3. disloyal
PERFUNCTORY	1. obsolete	2. unenthusiastic	3. arrogant
PERSPICACIOUS	1. perceptive	2. wet	3. roundabout
PLAINTIVE	1. disagreeable	2. mournful	3. apparent
PRECIPITOUS	1. wet	2. steep	3. premature
PRECOCIOUS	1. snobby	2. rebellious	3. advanced
PREDILECTION	1. preference	2. forecast	3. regret
PROBITY	1. accuracy	2. honesty	3. curiosity
PRODIGIOUS	1. wasteful	2. early	3. enormous
PROFLIGATE	1. brave	2. wasteful	3. ominous
PROLIX	1. wordy	2. festive	3. productive
PROPINQUITY	1. mischief	2. nearness	3. seriousness
PROPITIATE	1. appease	2. command	3. possess
PUERILE	1. flexible	2. novel	3. childish
PULCHRITUDE	1. beauty	2. understanding	3. courage
PURITANICAL	1. strict	2. honorable	3. skeptical
PUSILLANIMOUS	1. lively	2. cowardly	3. generous
QUANDARY	1. assortment	2. celebration	3. dilemma
QUERULOUS	1. nervous	2. eccentric	3. complaining
QUIESCENT	1. inactive	2. harmonious	3. brilliant
QUIXOTIC	1. carefree	2. hesitant	3. idealistic
RAPACIOUS	1. talkative	2. greedy	3. deceitful
RECALCITRANT	1. creative	2. stubborn	3. respectful
RECTITUDE	1. honor	2. perspective	3. solitude
REPINE	1. complain	2. yearn	3. surmise
REPUDIATE	1. congratulate	2. reject	3. liberate
RESPITE	1. feud	2. pause	3. isolation
RESTIVE	1. relaxed	2. charming	3. restless
SACROSANCT	1. vigilant	2. proper	3. sacred
SAGACIOUS	1. daring	2. showy	3. wise
SALUBRIOUS	1. courteous	2. gullible	3. healthful
SATIATE	1. delay	2. satisfy	3. contaminate
SATURNINE	1. gloomy	2. brilliant	3. mystical
SEDULOUS	1. nomadic	2. shocking	3. diligent
SOLICITUDE	1. annoyance	2. ambition	3. concern

SOMNOLENT	1. gloomy	2. sleepy	3. confident
SOPHOMORIC	1. powerful	2. immature	3. truthful
SOPORIFIC	1. sleepy	2. naive	3. outstanding
SPECIOUS	1. cautious	2. pertinent	3. deceptive
SPLENETIC	1. irritable	2. barbaric	3. excited
SPORTIVE	1. disobedient	2. playful	3. competitive
SQUALID	1. filthy	2. violent	3. wasteful
STENTORIAN	1. sociable	2. disciplined	3. thunderous
STRIDENT	1. swift	2. harsh	3. constant
SUCCINCT	1. concise	2. prosperous	3. nearby
SUPERCILIOUS	1. outstanding	2. arrogant	3. luxurious
SUPPLICATE	1. banish	2. liberate	3. beg
SURFEIT	1. secrecy	2. surplus	3. falsehood
SURLY	1. dreary	2. confident	3. grouchy
SURREPTITIOUS	1. secretive	2. emotional	3. imitative
SYCOPHANT	1. flatterer	2. nonconformist	3. genius
SYLVAN	1. universal	2. wooded	3. ideal
TIRADE	1. ecstasy	2. adventure	3. reprimand
TOADY	1. flatterer	2. nonbeliever	3. newcomer
TORPID	1. logical	2. sluggish	3. angry
TRANSITORY	1. irrelevant	2. compatible	3. temporary
TRUCULENT	1. triumphant	2. persistent	3. belligerent
TRUNCATE	1. shorten	2. complicate	3. annihilate
TUMID	1. swollen	2. peaceful	3. sturdy
TURBID	1. accurate	2. muddy	3. hollow
TURGID	1. chaotic	2. concise	3. swollen
UBIQUITOUS	1. talkative	2. suitable	3. everywhere
UPBRAID	1. scold	2. liberate	3. improve
VENERATE	1. participate	2. worship	3. stimulate
VERBOSE	1. original	2. wordy	3. educational
VERDANT	1. lush	2. sarcastic	3. truthful
VERITABLE	1. diverse	2. actual	3. praiseworthy
VICARIOUS	1. indirect	2. strenuous	3. elegant
VILIFY	1. astonish	2. instruct	3. slander
VIRULENT	1. muscular	2. poisonous	3. tranquil
VITRIOLIC	1. productive	2. enthusiastic	3. sarcastic
VOLUBLE	1. voluntary	2. talkative	3. urgent
VORACIOUS	1. ravenous	2. timid	3. jealous
WINSOME	1. patient	2. triumphant	3. charming
WIZENED	1. informed	2. annoyed	3. shriveled

Index

about the author – 5
alternate approach (*see* strategies)
analogies – 26-41
   (*also see* strategies)
   quiz – 29-34, 37-40
   quiz answers explained – 30, 32, 34, 39-40
   "ship list" – 33

books helpful for SAT strategy/skill-building:
   10 Real SATs – 133, 184
   Penny Press Puzzles – 48, 132, 133, 184
   The Karelitz SAT Dictionary of One-Word Definitions – 18,132, 133, 184
   The New Millennium Power Dictionary – 184
   The New SAT In Ten Easy Steps – 3, 133, 184

calculator – 68, 74, 79, 96
closing note by the author – 133-134
college "trump" cards – 8
colleges and the **SAT** – 8
column comparisons (math) – 86-101
   (*also see* strategies)
   quiz – 89-90, 93-99
   quiz answers explained – 89-90, 97-99
computer program, *Verbal/Math Vanquish* – 184
concentration – 48
concise review (math) – 136, 138
concise review (verbal) – 135, 137
crossword puzzles – 17, 49, 132, 133, 184

final exam – 139-178
   answers – 178
   scoring chart – 180
final thought – 25, 41, 59, 81, 101, 114, 115, 131
"finger-strategy" (*see* speed-reading)

grids-in (math) – 102-114
   (*also see* strategies)
   quiz – 108-112
   quiz answers explained – 110-112

guessing – 44

integer – 65

The Karelitz SAT Dictionary of One-Word Definitions – 18, 132, 133, 184

limited elimination (*see* strategies)
logic problems – 49, 132
long-term improvement, suggestions – 19, 35, 49, 80, 100, 113, 124, 182-183

math section – 60-64
   (*also see* multiple choice, grid-ins, and column comparisons)
maximizing SAT scores – 12, 14, 17, 18, 59, 64, 67, 78, 115, 137, 138
mean – 110
median – 110
minimum/maximum problems – 76, 84, 85
"missing link" strategy (*see* "purpose"strategy)
mode – 110
multiple choice (math) – 66-85
   (*also see* strategies)
   quiz – 70-77
   quiz answers explained – 74-77
myths/facts – 10, 12, 13, 14, 41, 42, 43, 44, 46, 47, 60, 61, 62, 66, 90, 91, 104, 105

overview (math) – 64
overview (verbal) – 13

"practice makes perfect" advice (math) – 64
preface – 3-6
PSAT test of writing skills (*see* test of writing skills)
"purpose" strategy (analogies) – 28, 29

quantitative comparison (*see* column comparisons)
quizzes (*see* under specific section)

reading – 42-59
  (*also see* strategies)
  quiz – 50-58
  quiz answers explained – 55-58
recommended books/video/computer program
– 184
review:
  analogies – 35
  column comparisons – 100
  grid-ins – 113
  multiple choice (math) – 80
  reading – 49
  sentence completions – 19
  test of writing skills (**PSAT**) – 123

same/opposite (analogies) – 27, 32
SAT final exam (*see* final exam)
SAT II – 2, 61, 117, 131
scoring – 12, 78
  (*also see* strategies)
sentence completions – 14-25
  (*also see* strategies)
  quiz – 21-24
  quiz answers explained – 23-24
skill-building prep quiz (math) – 82-85
slope – 97
speed-reading – 45
strategies:
  alternate approach – 78
  analogies – 27-34
  column comparisons – 87-91
  grid-ins – 103-105
  limited elimination – 16, 47
  maximum scoring – 12, 59, 64, 137-138
  multiple choice (math) – 69
  overall review – 135, 181
  reading – 45-47
  sentence completions – 15-18
  strategy-review checklist – 181
  test of writing skills (**PSAT**) – 118-120
student-produced answers (*see* grid-ins)
suggestions for long-term improvement:
  analogies – 35
  column comparisons – 100

general **SAT** – 182-183
grid-ins – 113
math (general) – 183
multiple choice (math) – 80
reading – 49
sentence completions – 19
test of writing skills – 123
verbal (general) – 182

test of writing skills – 117-131
  (*also see* strategies)
  quiz – 120-122, 124-130
  quiz answers explained – 122, 130
thesaurus – 17, 132, 184
time – 19, 35, 48, 49, 66, 80, 100, 113, 123,
135, 136
troubleshooting – 182-183
TWS (*see* test of writing skills)

verbal section – 13
  (*also see* sentence completions, analogies,
  and reading)
video, 2 hour **SAT**-review – 184
vocabulary quizzes – 189-194, 198-203
vocabulary word lists – 17, 18
  (*also see* word-list)

"weighted average" – 76
word-list: 480 **SAT** words – 185-203
writing skills (*see* test of writing skills)

A Better Way
to Test
Problem-Solving Skills:

(a personal observation by the author)

A CROSSWORD PUZZLE/LOGIC PUZZLE TEST would measure the same skills that the SAT now attempts to measure. It would challenge students to put their problem-solving skills to task and would invariably provide colleges with what they really want: an assessment of students' thinking skills.